Companion to
THE ROBERT AND KERSTIN ADAMS
PHOTOGRAPHY COLLECTION
at the Denver Art Museum

CONTENTS

FOREWORD

The gift of the Robert and Kerstin Adams Collection was an exciting development in the long and mutually engaging relationship between the Adamses and the Denver Art Museum. Before Robert Adams thought seriously about photography—and long before he became one of the most prominent and influential photographers of the late twentieth century—he visited the museum with his sister Carolyn to look at paintings during breaks from their studies at Wheat Ridge High School in suburban Denver. Roughly twenty years later, the museum was proud to publish his fourth book, *Prairie*, in conjunction with a 1978 solo exhibition of his photographs from eastern Colorado. In the years since then, the museum has mounted three more solo exhibitions of Adams's work and built a collection of more than 160 of his photographs.

The Adams Collection is a rich and intriguing mix of photographs where masterworks by well-known historical and contemporary figures sit elbow-to-elbow with snapshots and photo postcards by people whose names we will never know. They reflect, to some extent, how the couple's interests evolved from the time when Robert was an English professor at Colorado College, through the twenty-six years they lived in Longmont (where Kerstin was a reference librarian at the public library), and to the twenty-four years and counting they have spent overlooking the Columbia River from their home in Astoria, Oregon. For as long as fifty years, these pictures have delighted and sustained Robert and Kerstin in their everyday lives, their environmental activism, and the pursuit of their creative work. It could not have been easy for them to say goodbye. The museum is honored to hold these artworks in its permanent collection, and I would like to thank Eric Paddock for his thoughtful selection of photographs to include here. This companion guide introduces readers to about a quarter of the overall collection and expresses, in its small way, the museum's enduring gratitude for Robert and Kerstin's generous gift.

Christoph Heinrich
Frederick and Jan Mayer Director

INTRODUCTION

Your own photography is never enough. Every photographer who has lasted has depended on other people's pictures too—photographs that may be public or private, serious or funny, but that carry with them a reminder of community. —Robert Adams

Forming a collection of photographs is something like making and keeping friends. Collectors gravitate toward certain kinds of photographs in much the way we are drawn to certain kinds of people for their honesty or courage, their ideals, their humor, their trustworthiness, or sometimes just their looks. Finding a good match requires a bit of sifting; keeping the relationship alive requires attention to what the photograph has to say and openness to the wisdom it offers over time. Robert and Kerstin Adams began collecting in a modest way sixty years ago; their collection evolved to reflect the values that shaped their work as artists and activists and the wide community of artists who have nurtured, followed, or grown alongside them.

The photographs and other artworks in the Adams Collection arrived in a variety of ways. The couple bought a few things early on. As they came to know more photographers and Robert's reputation grew, many pictures came through trades with colleagues while others simply fell through the mail slot—gifts from strangers who sought encouragement for their work or who wanted to acknowledge the creative and ethical integrity of the Adamses' exemplary work. By whatever means they arrived, the photographs that stayed did triple duty in the Adams household, offering private pleasures as individual artworks, focusing conversations with visitors, and standing as tokens of friendship and mutual respect. As Robert Adams suggests, the collection provided the comfort—at both ends of these exchanges—of knowing one is not alone.

Robert and Kerstin married in 1960.[1] Living in Colorado Springs, where Robert was an English professor at Colorado College, the Adamses took frequent jaunts through the hinterlands of Colorado and northern New Mexico. Robert began using a 35 mm camera to photograph nature and architecture on those trips. He learned darkroom techniques from Colorado Springs photographer Myron Wood and found early inspiration in volumes of Alfred Stieglitz's *Camera Work*, *This Is the American Earth* by Ansel Adams (no relation), and issues of the photography journal *Aperture*.[2] These and photographs by other artists helped to shape the vision Adams demonstrated in his early photography books about Colorado's landscape, its traditional architecture, and its burgeoning suburbs.

Learning from the creative successes of others is essential to every artist's understanding of what they hope to do. On a visit to the Denver Art Museum around 1970, Robert Adams encountered a small painting by Worthington Whittredge that has resonated with him for fifty years. *Foothills Colorado* (fig. 1) is an 1870 study of the Front Range near present-day Longmont, Colorado; it looks across the St. Vrain Creek to the dry foothills below what is now Rocky Mountain National Park. Working in flat light on a warm summer day, Whittredge made a convincing picture of what is, by today's standards, an unremarkable

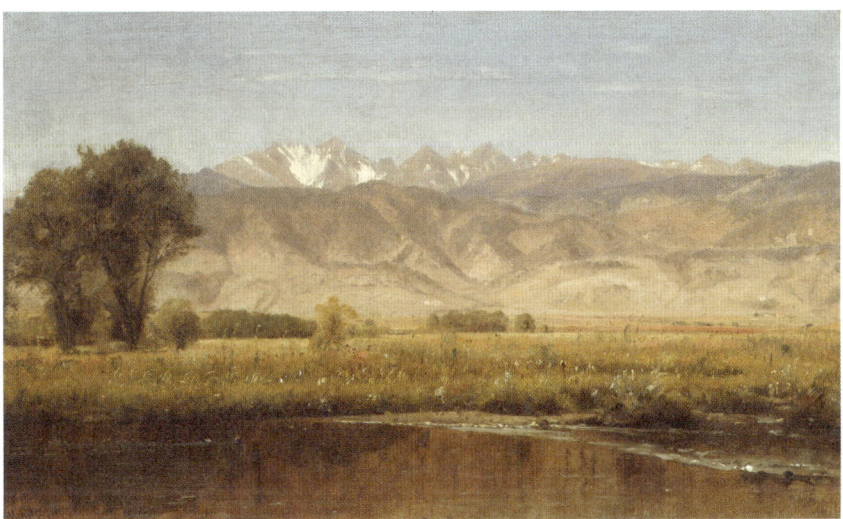

Fig. 1 Worthington Whittredge, *Foothills Colorado*, about 1870. Oil paint on paper; 11¾ × 19¾ in. (29.8 × 50.2 cm). Partial gift of the Houston Foundation in memory of M. Elliott and funds from various donors by exchange, 1969.160.

scene. It is the kind of place and moment that a painter of Whittredge's skill, or a well-traveled Coloradan and photographer like Adams, is likely to appreciate. The painting reminded Adams of the beauty he experienced on his own youthful rambles in the West. For him, the silence and emptiness of Whittredge's scene, painted almost a century before Adams saw it, stood in stark contrast to the burgeoning population, expanding industrial landscapes, and urban sprawl Adams observed every day. He later said the painting inspired confidence in his own vision and reminded him that simple, direct pictures speak in ways that contrived ones never do.[3]

A drawing by the artist Richard Serra (fig. 2) further illustrates how artists who work in different mediums can find shared understanding in each other's work. One would not expect an artist known for colossal steel sculptures and one who makes small, tonally nuanced photographs to find common ground; even so, when Robert learned through a mutual friend that Serra's house contained almost no artworks apart from several of Robert's photographs, he ventured to

Fig. 2 Richard Serra, *Composite*, 2016. Litho crayon and ink on handmade paper; 13 × 18¼ in. (33 × 46.4 cm). Gift of Kerstin and Robert Adams, 2018.439.

send a recent picture of an Oregon forest to Serra's studio. A large package arrived on the Adamses' doorstep a short time later; they were delighted to find Serra's drawing—a picture suggesting a forest as dense and full of light and shadow as Robert's photograph.[4] The exchange demonstrates the goodwill and respect that creative people can show to one another.

In the early 1960s, the Adamses purchased carefully selected photographs, including a Yousuf Karsh portrait of the Swedish diplomat Dag Hammarskjöld (fig. 3). The portrait had special meaning because, like Hammerskjöld, Kerstin was born in Sweden, but it was also a reminder to keep alive the steadfast commitment to world peace Hammarskjöld demonstrated as Secretary-General of the United Nations from 1953 to 1961. For Robert and Kerstin, the portrait may have represented the need to apply personal aspirations toward a common good.

If the Hammarskjöld portrait served as an ethical avatar, a carving of San Miguel (fig. 4) related more directly to work in hand. Purchased on one of their many photography trips to southern Colorado and northern New Mexico, this *santo* connected them to the cultural dimensions of subjects Robert was photographing in the field. Several photographs of carved saints appear in the 1974 book *The Architecture and Art of Early Hispanic Colorado*, as do photographs similar to *Our Lady of Guadalupe Chapel, Medina Plaza, Colorado* (fig. 5)—the only photo by Robert in the Adams Collection.[5] Showing religious artworks together with examples of vernacular structures in the landscapes was the Adamses' way of honoring the traditional crafts of Hispanic settlements that predated settlement from the eastern United States. Having the santo in their house for years afterward reminded them of their adventures and kept their respect alive.[6]

Several photographs in the Adams Collection show a lightheartedness or humor. Certainly the old snapshots and some of the real photo post-cards in the collection were meant to be funny, or at least strike us that way now; Lee Friedlander's photograph (p. 31) of firemen smiling for a group portrait in front of a burning house is a marvelous lampoon of every solemn group portrait that has ever been made. Humor in photography is precious because it reminds us to take ourselves less

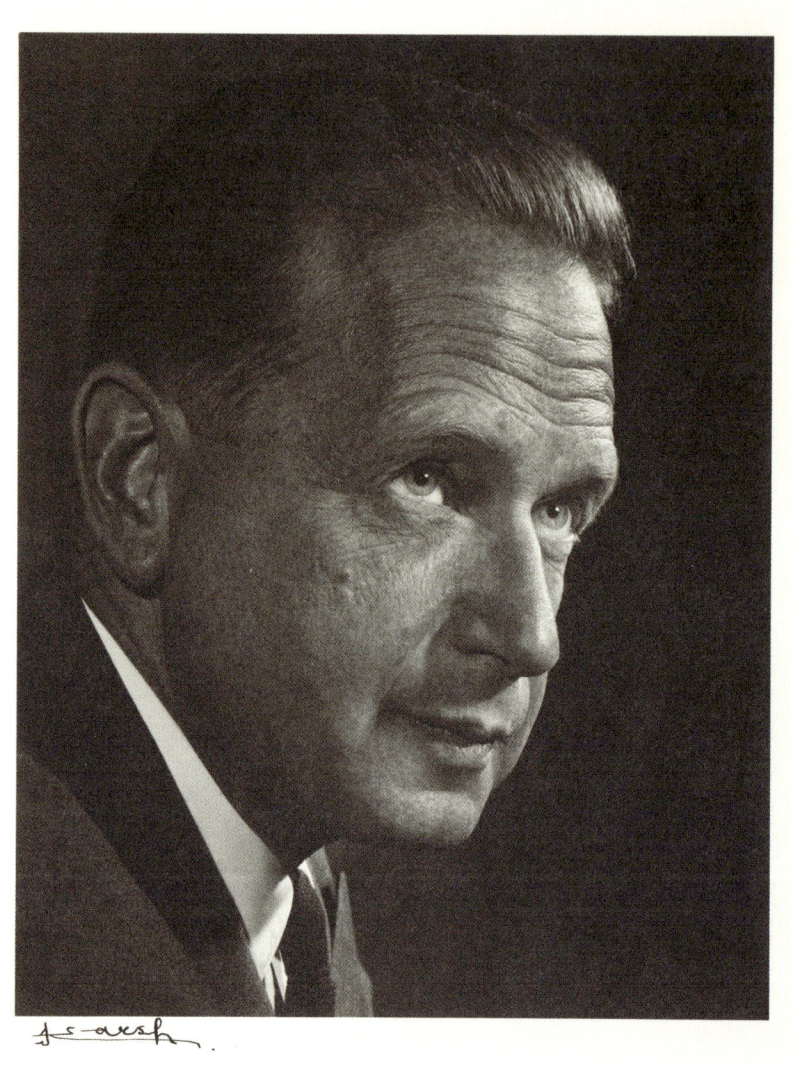

Fig. 3 Yousuf Karsh, *Dag Hammarskjöld*, 1958. Gelatin silver print; 9½ × 7½ in. (24.1 × 19.1 cm). Gift of Kerstin and Robert Adams, 2018.502.

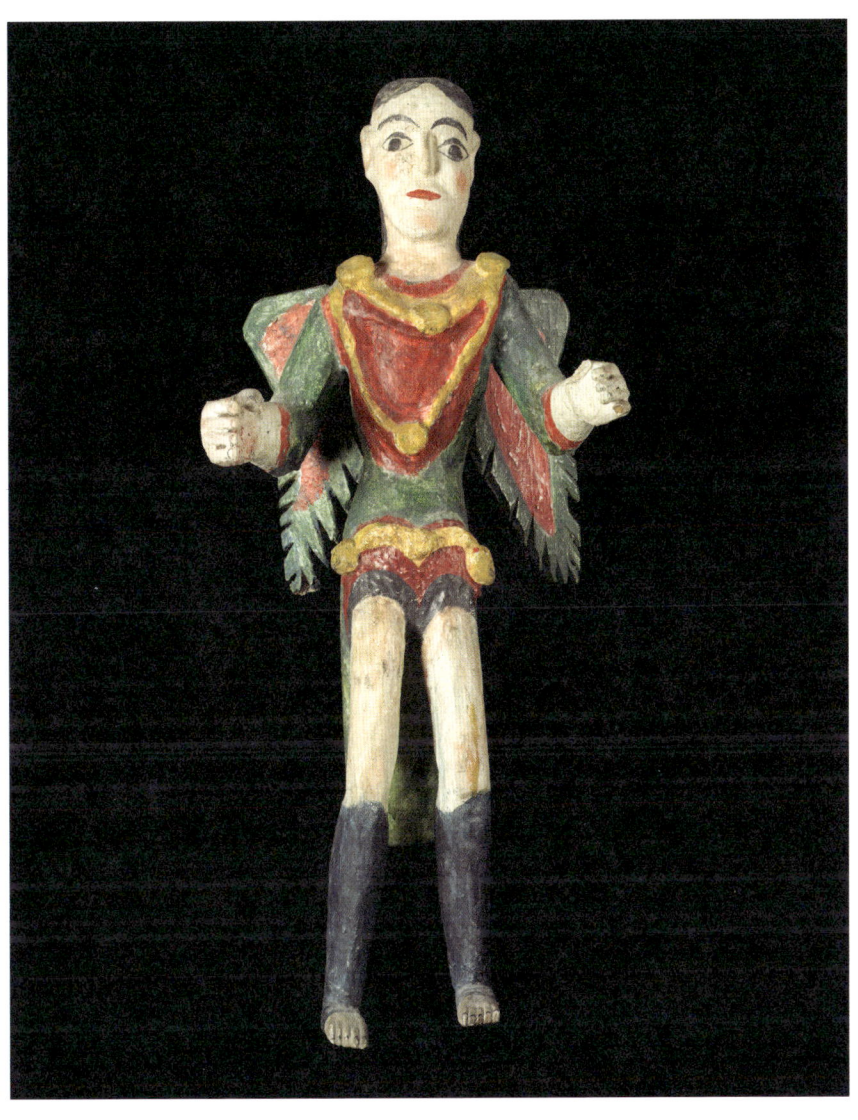

Fig. 4 Unknown maker, *San Miguel*, 1800s. Carved and painted wood; 22 × 10 × 8¼ in. (55.9 × 25.4 × 21 cm). Gift of Kerstin and Robert Adams, 2018.436.

seriously for a little while and because laughter in the face of one photograph can add depth to more serious images. Nicholas Nixon's 1975 photograph of the Adamses' female airedale, Fred, in their first Longmont backyard (fig. 6) commemorates the photographer's first meeting with them, the laughter they shared, and Nixon's fond childhood memory of another airedale.[7]

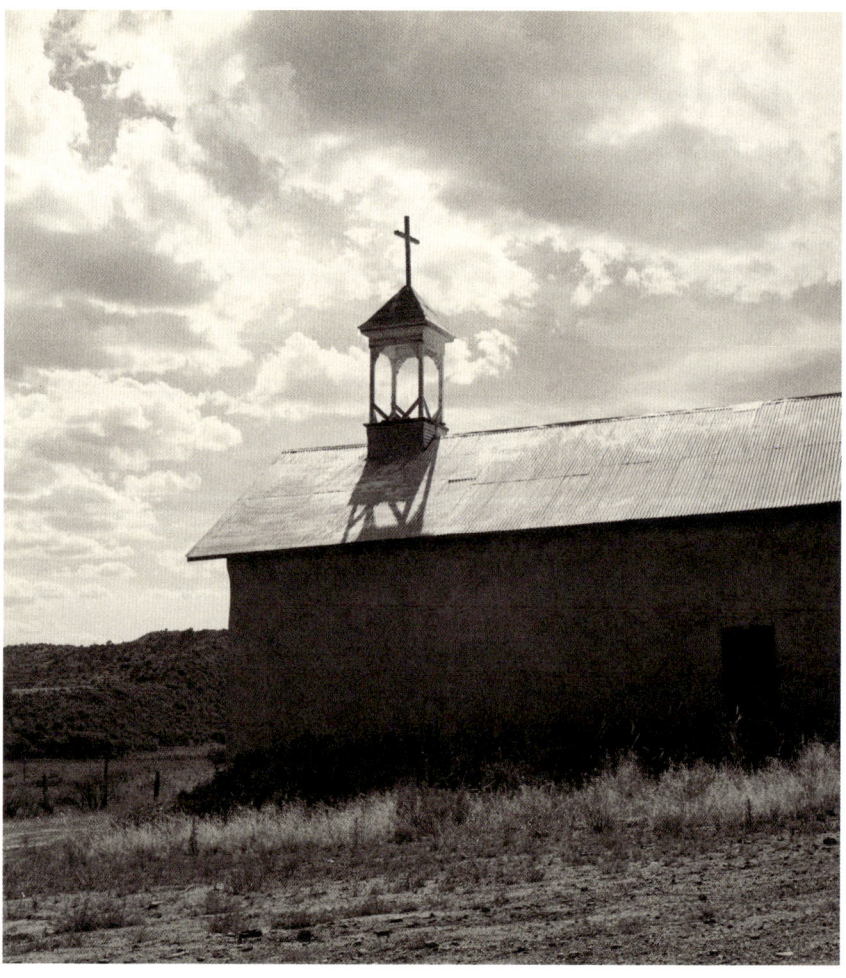

Fig. 5   Robert Adams, *Our Lady of Guadalupe Chapel, Medina Plaza, Colorado*, 1971. Gelatin silver print; $8^{7}/_{8}$ × $8^{3}/_{8}$ in. (22.5 × 21.3 cm). Gift of Kerstin and Robert Adams, 2018.440.

Photographers often speak of the value—the necessity—of "living with" a picture before judging its success or failure. While heading to the refrigerator or searching for one's keys, one might notice something in a photograph that could go unseen otherwise. Living with a picture in this way invites the familiarity, even the intimate knowledge, of a good friendship. Like the best companions, the photographs in the Adams Collection gave Robert and Kerstin much to ponder as well as much to enjoy over the many years that they held them in their home. Evidence of kindred spirits working across time and distance, they outline, in pictures, the community of photographers that has sustained them and inspired them to carry on in their own great work.

Eric Paddock
Curator of Photography

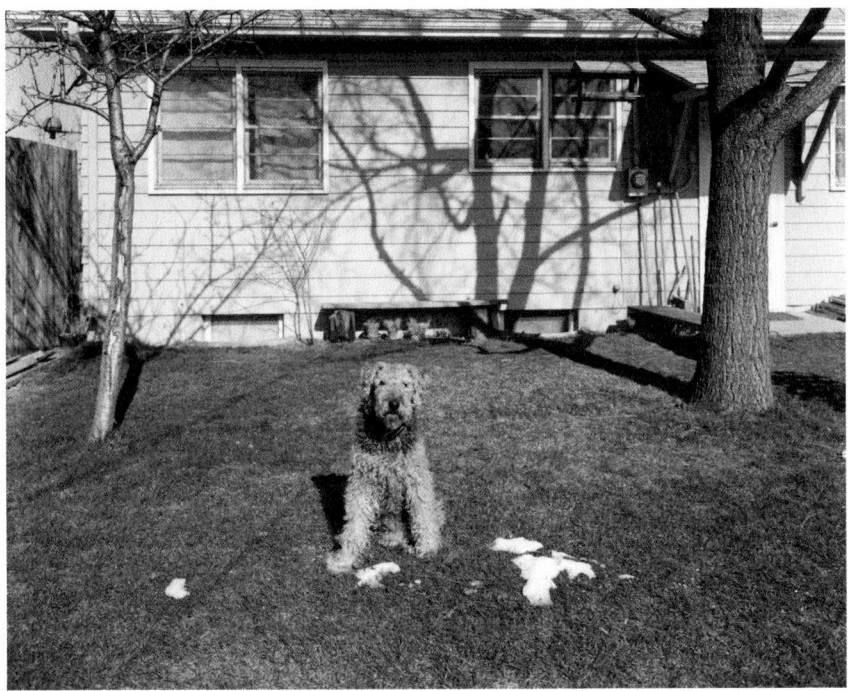

Fig. 6 Nicholas Nixon, *Longmont, Colorado,* 1975. Gelatin silver print; 8 × 10 in. (20.3 × 25.4 cm). Gift of Kerstin and Robert Adams, 2018.510.

NOTES

Epigraph: Robert Adams, "Colleagues," *Why People Photograph* (New York: Aperture, 1994), 13.

[1] A detailed chronology of Robert Adams's life and career before 2010 appears in the unpaginated exhibition catalog *Robert Adams: The Place We Live, a Retrospective Selection of Photographs, 1964–2009*, vol. 3 (New Haven: Yale University Press, 2011). That publication accompanied a retrospective exhibition of over 300 photographs presented at the Vancouver Art Gallery; the Denver Art Museum; the Museo Nacional Centro de Arte Reina Sofía in Madrid; the Josef Albers Museum in Bottrop, Germany; the Galerie du Jeu de Paume in Paris; and the Yale University Art Gallery in New Haven, Connecticut.

[2] See note 1. Adams was fortunate to find original volumes of *Camera Work* and *Aperture* in the library of the Colorado Springs Fine Art Center and to receive a copy of the Ansel Adams book as a gift. Although this companion guide is focused on photographic prints, one cannot understate the importance of photography books and serial publications in fostering an awareness of community in the hearts of working photographers.

[3] Robert Adams, in multiple conversations with the author, 1984–2010.

[4] Robert Adams, in conversations with the author, 2018 and 2021.

[5] The Denver Art Museum holds more than 160 Robert Adams photographs acquired from other sources.

[6] Robert Adams, in conversation with the author, 2017.

[7] Adams, "Colleagues," 13.

There is something oddly compelling about looking at old family photos of strangers. Our connection with the individuals in pictures like these is not personal—we don't look at them in the same way we view our own family photos. Instead, they come to represent shared aspects of human relationships and experiences. Despite the space, time, and circumstances that may divide the viewer from the people in this picture, we can relate to the act of gathering with loved ones to commemorate a treasured moment or event.

This whimsical family photo set within a field of daisies is filled with charm. The photograph may document a flower-picking outing, or maybe they stumbled upon this field in bloom while en route elsewhere and simply could not pass up the photo op. Given that they are dressed up, it seems most likely this was a planned location for a family photo. The car in the background, the bunches of flowers in their hands, the single flower in the scarf of the woman in the dark-colored dress, all provoke the viewer to ponder the series of actions leading up to and following this moment.

People have had the desire to memorialize important moments in photographs since the medium was introduced. Today, the camera is more present in daily life than ever before—many people have cameras built into their phones and can take a picture at any time. A hundred years ago, when this photo was made, far fewer snapshots were taken because the materials were more expensive and not as widely available as they are today. As a result, the occasion for a photograph took on greater significance, and the physical prints that survive are even more precious. Will strangers one hundred years from now look at the countless digital family photos taken today with quite the same affection?

KR

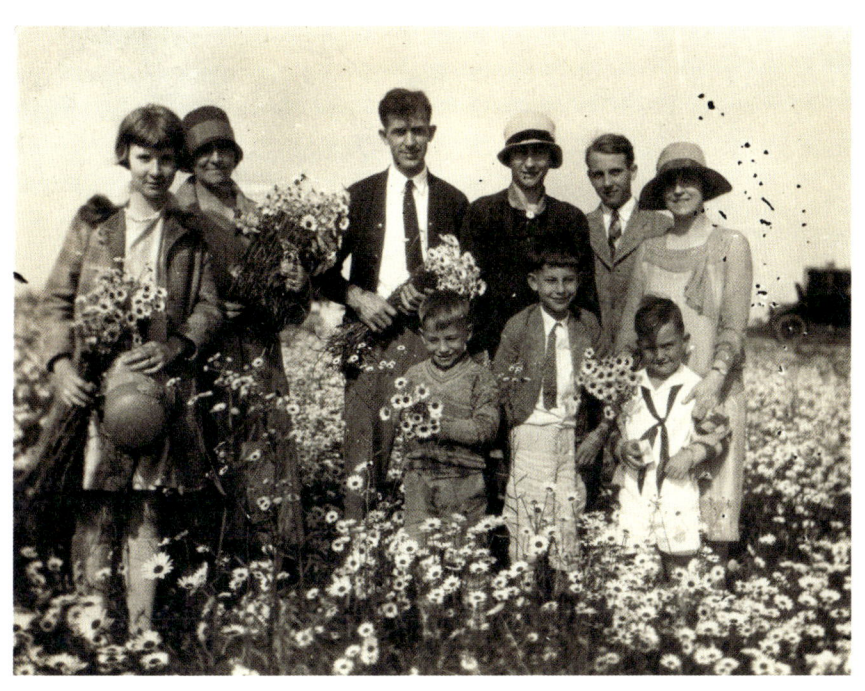

Unknown maker
Family Group with Flowers
1920s
Gelatin silver print
3 × 4 in. (7.6 × 10.2 cm)
2018.574

The Kodak camera was introduced by George Eastman and the Eastman Dry Plate and Film Company (later Eastman Kodak Company) in 1888. It was the first handheld camera available that was designed to make photography more accessible to the general public. The Kodak cost $25 at the time (equivalent to $700 today) and came loaded with a one hundred-exposure roll of flexible film, also recently created by the company. Once the roll of film was finished, the whole camera could be sent to the factory in Rochester, New York, where the film was developed, prints were made, and new film could be loaded before returning to the customer. Advertised with the slogan, "You press the button, we do the rest," the Kodak greatly simplified the process of photography, which sparked the rise of the amateur photographer and the everyday snapshots we are so accustomed to today. It still took a few more years for the camera to become more affordable, but from this point forward, photography would become increasingly present in our lives.

The first model of this handheld box camera created round photographs such as this one. The circular format of the picture echoes the shape of the child's sun hat and the wheels of the wagon. The house on the right, with the attached clothesline, leads the eye to the crop field in the distance, providing context for the central scene: a young girl playing with her furry friends outside a rural home. Like many children, this girl sought entertainment and companionship in her pets and toys. Here, she has placed her stuffed teddy bear and doll in a wagon along with her patient and willing dog while she clutches her cat as if preparing for an adventure. The photographer, likely a family member or friend, recognized the picture-worthy moment and captured this humorous scene of childhood play, so it could be remembered and enjoyed for years to come.

KR

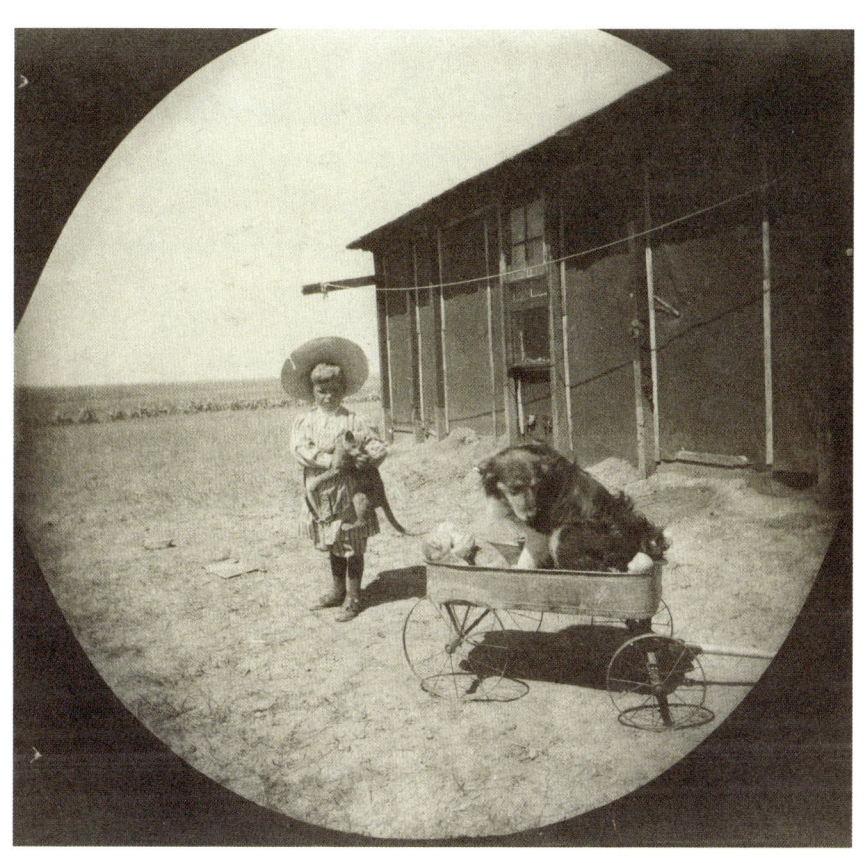

Unknown maker
Child, Wagon, and Dog
1890s
Gelatin silver print
4 in. (10.2 cm) dia.
2018.575

What we now call real photo postcards emerged after 1907, when Congress and the U.S. Postal Service authorized the use of photographic paper for postcards. That simple policy shift sparked a flourishing trade in homemade photographs that could be sent any-where in the country for a penny—the cost of a stamp. No longer were consumers confined to the predictable imagery offered by traditional ink-on-paper publishers. Drugstores and photo finishers offered postcard-sized prints; serious amateurs made their own. The craze slowed during the Great Depression and all but disappeared when the government reserved photographic materials for military use during World War II. Consumers flocked to color photography after the war, urged on by aggressive marketing campaigns by Eastman Kodak and the rising popularity of color television.

The practical beauty of the postcard was that one could write an address and short message on the back of any picture, affix a stamp, and send it on its way. Local mail could reach its destination the same day it was sent, making the postcard a quick and easy way to spread gossip or invite a friend to dinner in areas—and there were many—where there was no telephone service. In that way, postcards paved the way for ever-faster communication, culminating, for now, in text messages and social media such as TikTok and Instagram. Together, the pictures and messages of real photo postcards allow us to see into the private worlds of ordinary people and paint the vernacular history of early-twentieth-century life.

These examples, by unknown amateur photographers, offer glimpses of life on the American prairie. Two women, posed at the foot of a windmill in a snow-covered landscape, seem a bit stiff in their long skirts and white blouses as they squint into the glare of the surrounding country-side. A little boy also squints a bit and smiles directly into the lens while a collie keeps watch, a group of adults engages in a tug-o-war, and the high plains roll out behind him. Although the private significance of small moments like these, frozen in time, is unknowable, the pictures invite a kind of fellow-feeling that connects us with the past and with each other.

EP

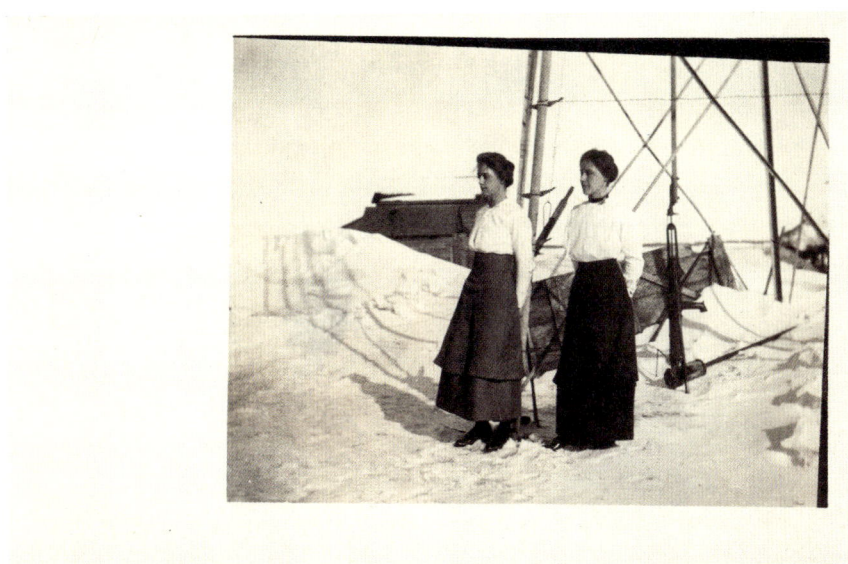

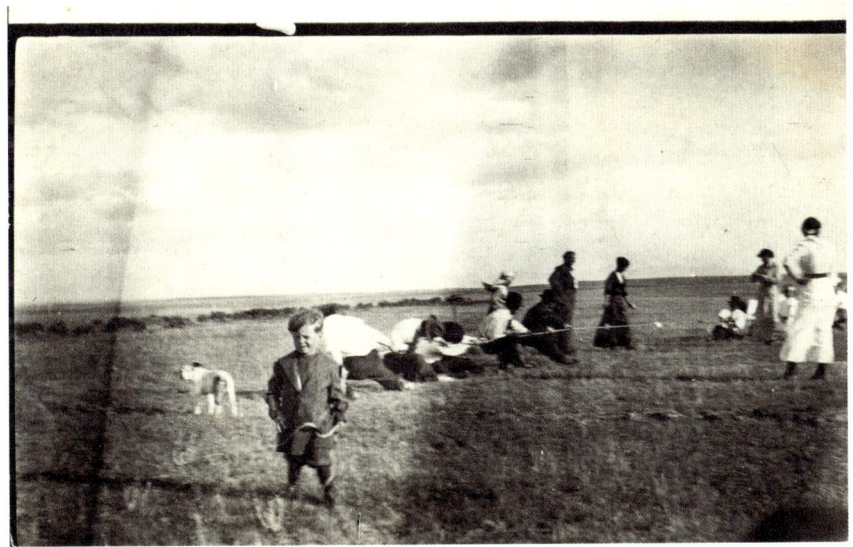

Unknown makers
Real Photo Postcard (Two Women)
1904–18
Real Photo Postcard (Boy, Dog, Tug-o-war)
1904–1920s
Gelatin silver prints
Each postcard 3½ × 5½ in. (8.9 × 14 cm)
2018.540-.541

The top photograph here is a bit of a puzzle. Apart from the dark blotch in the upper right-hand corner, its crisp focus and nuanced tones recall the work of master photographers from the twentieth century. The trees, soft shade, and splashes of sunlight on the lawn offer a sense of tranquility. One can almost hear birdsong and the hum of bees. Probably made by a practiced, open-minded amateur, the photograph is a beautiful surprise in a modest package.

Although most real photo postcards appear to be the work of unsung amateurs, sometimes an enterprising person made postcard photography a sideline to their regular work. The card illustrated at the bottom of the opposite page very likely was the work of a semiprofessional operator— either a local or someone who traveled from town to town by wagon or rail, working to order and delivering the pictures on a later trip.

Citizens of Gordon, Nebraska, undoubtedly took pride in the large stone hotel halfway down the block, the First National Bank with its $40,000 capital, and streets wide enough to easily turn a horse-drawn wagon. The block is framed by a jewelry and phonograph store and a cylindrical railroad water tower in the distance. There is one tree. Six men linger in the shade: three shopkeepers in white shirts and vests who look at the camera, two men chatting against a wall, and a thin cowboy who appears to have stopped to roll a cigarette. One can imagine buying this very photo in the hotel lobby and penciling a message to a friend.

EP

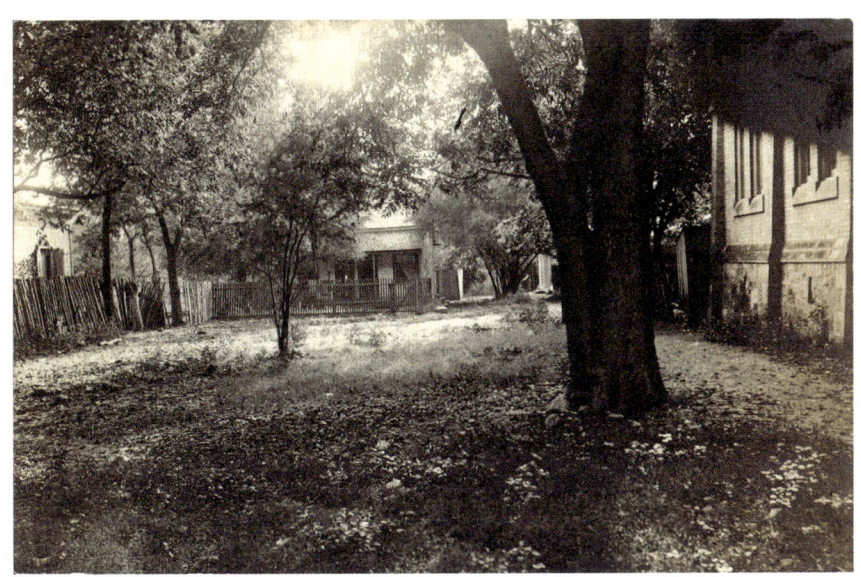

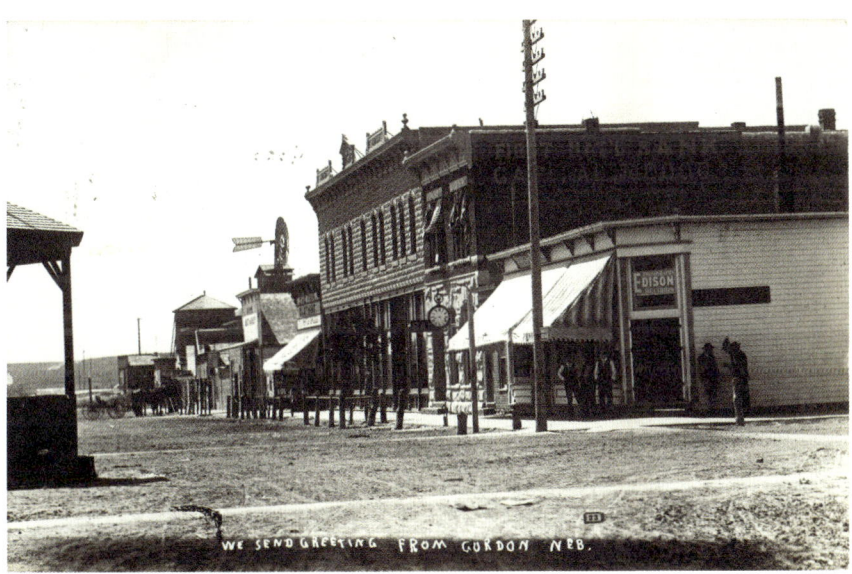

Unknown makers
Real Photo Postcard (Yard)
1900–10
Real Photo Postcard (We Send Greetings from Gordon, Neb.)
1907–08
Gelatin silver prints
Each postcard 3½ × 5½ in. (8.9 × 14 cm)
2018.548-.549

Dogs have won the hearts of photographers at least since the pioneering French photographers of the 1840s and 1850s posed them for studio portraits. They continue to touch us through William Wegman's slapstick pictures of Weimaraners and in heartbreaking photographs of stray or abused dogs by Fazal Sheikh, Alec Soth, and Martin Usborne. Robert Adams considered paintings and photographs by the artists Thomas Eakins and Pierre Bonnard in an essay devoted to dogs in art, concluding with the observation that "art depends on there being affection in its creator's life, and an artist must find ways, like everyone else, to nourish it. A photographer down on his or her knees picturing a dog has found pleasure enough to make many things possible." *

One of the beauties of real photo postcards was that people could send visual news updates to family and friends. Although "Squirrel Meets Dog" makes for a silly headline and hardly qualifies as breaking news, chances are that this postcard was made simply to bring a smile to those who received it. The picture speaks of the photographer's affection for animals and offers just the kind of pleasure Adams wrote about. The squirrel looks nervous and excited (as squirrels usually do); the dog seems mildly curious, yet just too comfortable to do anything but watch for a moment before it goes back to its nap.

EP

* Robert Adams, "Dogs," *Why People Photograph* (New York: Aperture, 1994), 51.

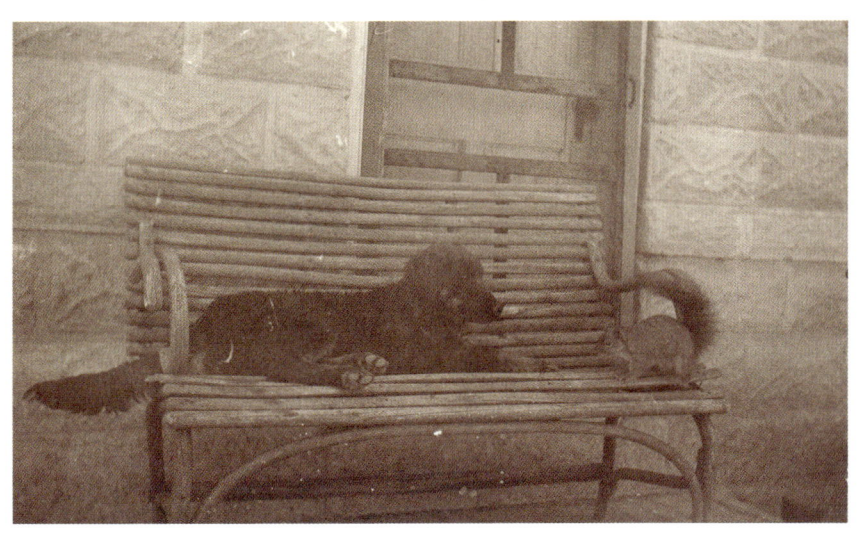

Unknown maker
Real Photo Postcard (Dog and Squirrel)
May 1910
Gelatin silver print
Postcard 3½ × 5½ in. (8.9 × 14 cm)
2018.544

From the early decades of the medium, photographers took cameras on their travels to all parts of the world and made pictures for personal and professional reasons. As cameras became more common, many people began to use them to document and memorialize their vacations. To this day, the average person probably takes the most pictures while traveling. Family photos and personal snapshots often serve as reminders of important events, experiences, and people in our lives. With time, we sometimes forget those moments until a photograph conjures it back to the surface of our memory and allows us to return to that time, even if for a moment.

These two snapshots document an outdoor excursion and, when viewed together, a story begins to unfold. In the first photo, a man returning from fishing proudly displays his catch, one fish in each hand. Here we see the reality of many snapshots—they don't always come out as intended. The photographer either hastily took the picture or, unknowingly, almost cut the fisherman's head out of the frame. The second photo shows two women enjoying a meal at their campsite. The canvas tent, foldable wooden furniture, and their cooking gear all suggest a comfortable camping experience. Hanging on the car just to the right of the spare tires are two fish, the same two fish being held by the man in the previous picture. He likely hung the fish on the car for dinner later, picked up the camera, and snapped this picture before joining the ladies for a meal.

KR

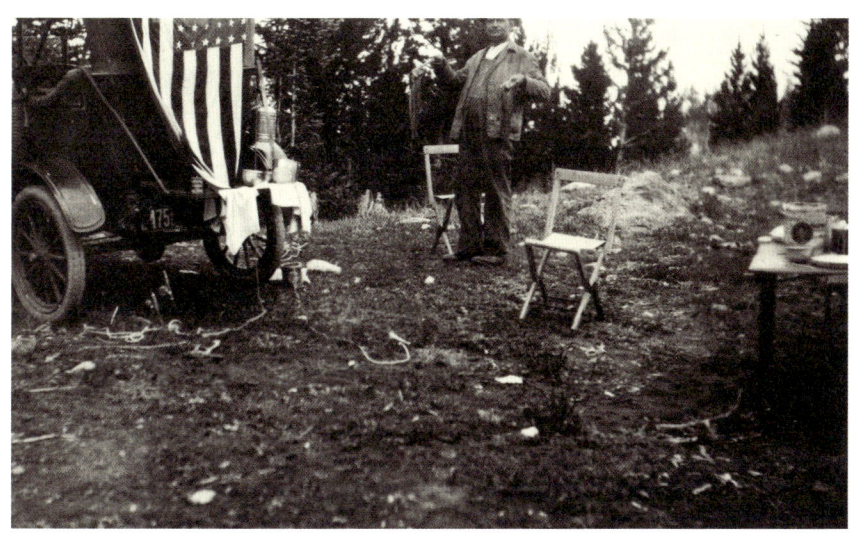

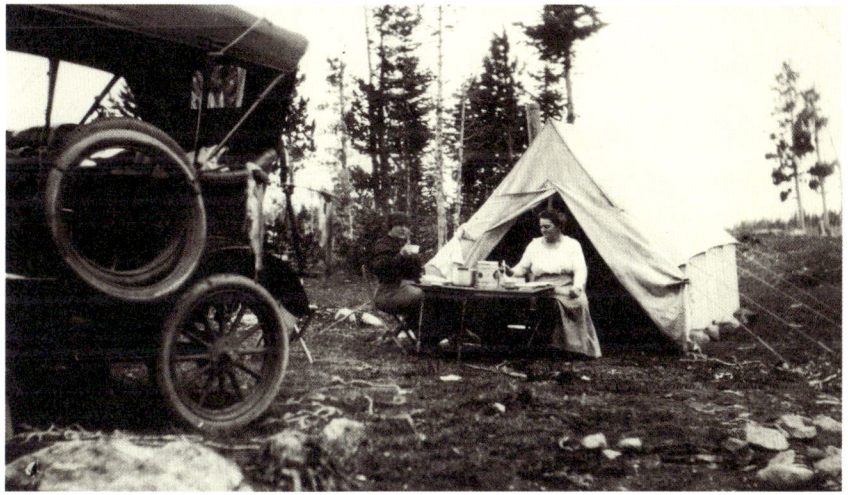

Unknown maker
Campsite with Car and U.S. Flag
Women, Tent, and Car
1910–25
Gelatin silver prints
Each 3⅛ × 5¼ in. (7.9 × 13.3 cm)
2018.577-.578

Robert Adams's grandfather, Charles Addison Hickman was an ardent amateur photographer active in South Dakota just before and after the turn of the twentieth century. His dedication to craft is evident in his choice of a five-by-eight-inch glass plate camera at a time when early point-and-shoot cameras captured a growing share of the market. Hickman set up a tripod, unfolded his camera, and composed and focused the picture before he slipped a plate holder into the camera back and released the shutter. After he got home and developed his negative, he brushed an iron-based solution onto a sheet of blank paper that he placed in sunlight with the negative on top; the result is this marvelous blue and white cyanotype print.

We don't know if the people in the foreground waited patiently while Hickman fussed with his camera gear or if they wandered into the frame as he worked to make a picture of the waterfall. Either way, the photograph suggests that he accepted what he was given and made the best of it. The boy in the tree, the woman steadying herself with her hand on a branch, the cows on the skyline, the harsh winter light, the rather scruffy-looking waterfall—the cartoon version would show the photographer spinning plates on sticks and juggling oranges while asking everyone to "please hold still!" And yet there is something refreshing, and something true, in the picture. Each person, each element contribute to a story of regular people enjoying an outing and stopping to commemorate the day in a photograph.

Nature photography as we know it today often focuses on unusual and spectacular scenery and seeks to convey an air of quiet solitude. Such idealized images of nature, experienced secondhand through photographs, create expectations that everyday life cannot always fulfill. A photograph like this one proposes that the pleasure of getting outside and connecting with nature does not require special clothing, expensive gear, or a jet to Kathmandu. Hickman touches on the simple enjoyment of whatever nature we find nearby and the contentment in sharing the experience of it with others.

EP

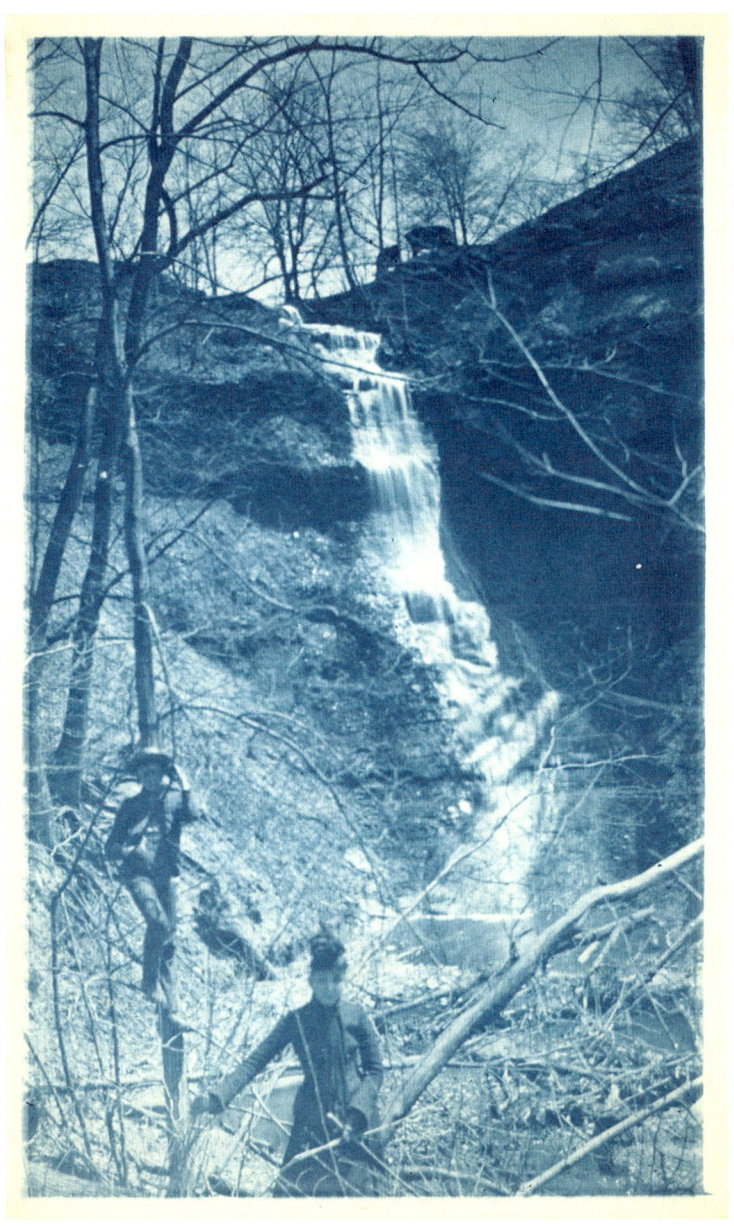

C. A. Hickman
American, 1875–1947
Waterfall
About 1900
Cyanotype
7½ × 4½ in. (19.1 × 11.4 cm)
2018.480

For the first forty years of photography's history, sitting for a portrait was a solemn and infrequent occasion, in part, because it required people to visit a photographer's studio and pay money for the experience. Acting out in front of the camera was uncommon until the 1880s, when portraits of, for example, playing poker with skeletons or coaxing dogs to do tricks became popular themes. All manner of high jinks appeared in pictures after George Eastman introduced his Kodak camera—a revolutionary point-and-shoot device that nearly anyone could use—in 1888, and the tradition thrives today.

Traces of the earlier solemnity persist in family snapshots that mark special occasions. At one time or another, most of us have been directed to stop and pose for a graduation snapshot or a group photo of some kind. Some of us are awkward and self-conscious in the circumstances while others take things in stride, and a few go hamming it up; usually, the resulting photos are less about the events they purport to celebrate than they are about the ritual performances of photographers and their subjects.

Lee Friedlander's photograph plays off of the snapshot ritual. At first glance, it is as flat-footed as a group portrait of children lined up on their school's front steps or of conventioneers standing next to a tour bus. But this squad of firefighters in full regalia is posed for its group portrait while the house behind them burns down! While it might be tempting to panic and shout, Friedlander's generous wit allows us to smile and shake our heads at the humanity of the situation.

EP

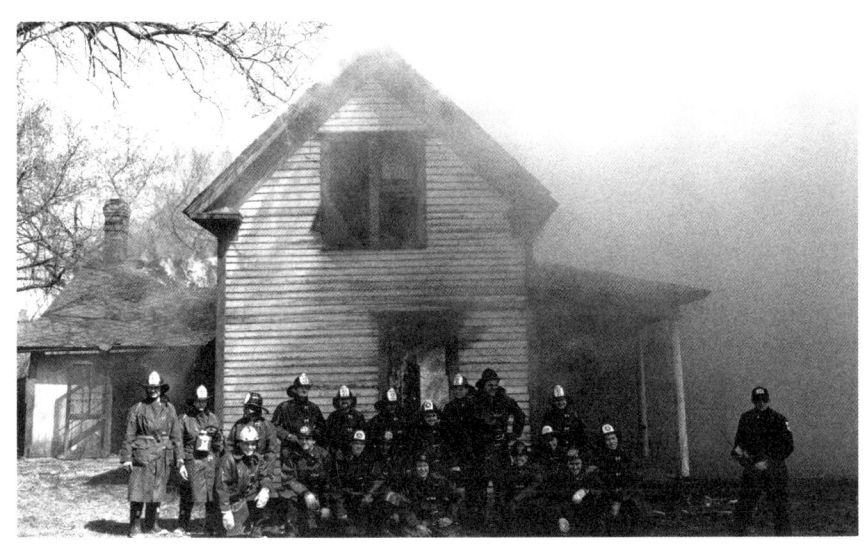

Lee Friedlander
American, born 1934
Minneapolis
1966
Gelatin silver print
6 × 9¼ in. (15.2 × 23.5 cm)
2018.472

Abraham Lincoln sat for this portrait by Mathew Brady on April 6, 1861, just one month after he was sworn in as the sixteenth president of the United States. The photograph suggests the intellectual strength and unbending moral authority that had carried Lincoln to the White House and, at the same time, records a fraught juncture in American history: already South Carolina and six other southern states had declared themselves a sovereign nation and elected Jefferson Davis as their president. Confederate forces opened fire on Fort Sumter in Charleston just six days after the picture was made. Lincoln would fall to an assassin's bullet four years later.

Sitting for Brady was a familiar rite of passage for American public figures. Brady learned photography from the inventor Samuel F. B. Morse, who was present when Louis Daguerre introduced his earth-changing photographic process at the Institut de France in 1839. His first New York studio opened in 1844 and soon attracted the political and cultural elite of the Eastern Seaboard, including John Quincy Adams, Andrew Jackson, Frederick Douglass, Walt Whitman, Sarah Bernhardt, and many others. No fewer than eighteen American presidents posed for Brady, as did most of the senior Union officers in the Civil War—and more than a few Confederate leaders who visited his premises before 1861. At the onset of the Civil War, he converted a wagon into a rolling darkroom and followed the Union army into the field; by 1864 he had employed at least twenty-three other photographers to take the risks while Brady—hampered, perhaps, by failing eyesight—directed their movements (and edited their work) from his Washington and New York studios.

Every known portrait of our sixteenth president was gathered together for a book entitled *The Face of Lincoln* (1979) ten years after the Civil Rights Act of 1968 became law. Richard Benson played a central role in the project, printing photographs from Brady's original glass plate negatives.

EP

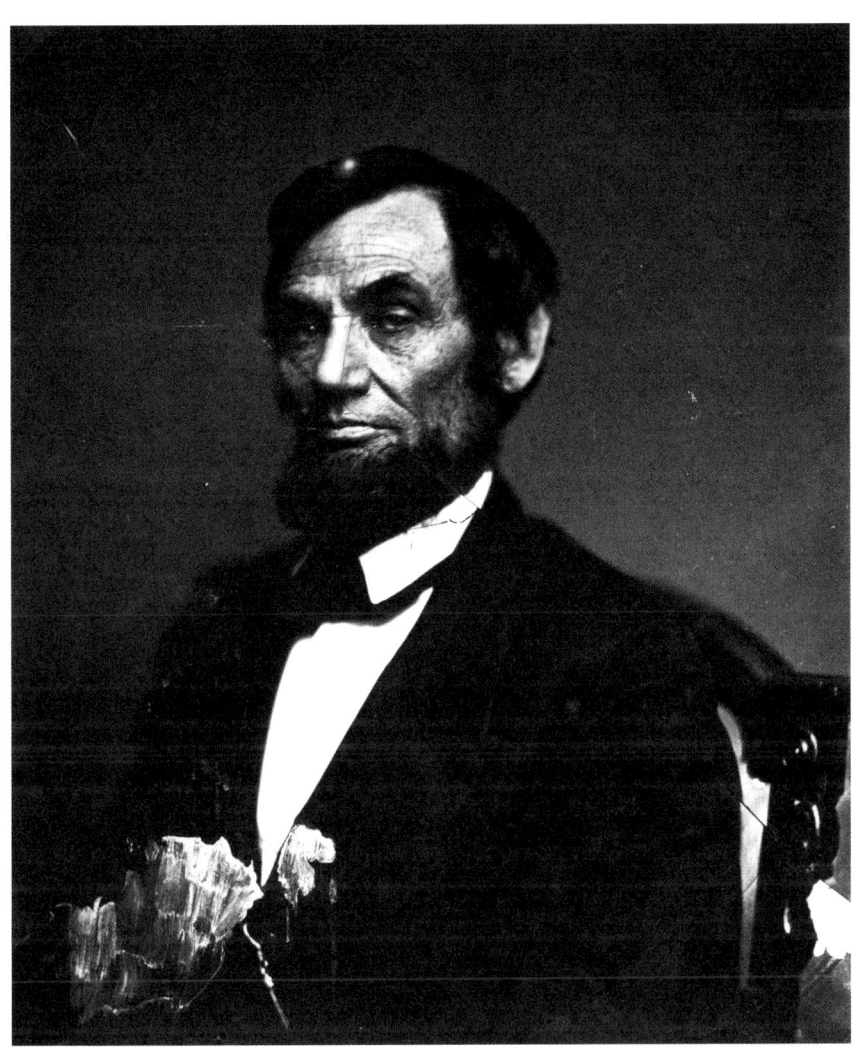

Mathew Brady
American, 1823–1896
Abraham Lincoln
April 6, 1861
Printed about 1970 by Richard Benson
Gelatin silver print
18⅝ × 15⅜ in. (47.3 × 39.1 cm)
2018.447

A. J. Meek learned photography in the U.S. Air Force (1963–67) and continued his studies in California before he earned his master of fine arts degree from Ohio University. He taught at Utah State University for five years, then settled into the art department at Louisiana State University in Baton Rouge, where he was Professor of Art from 1988 to his retirement in 2005. An aficionado of very large format cameras with negatives as large as twelve-by-twenty inches, Meek's process connects his work with nineteenth-century photographers who used similarly large cameras: John Horgan Jr., William Henry Jackson, and William H. Rau.

Documentary photography of regional subjects has been central to Meek's work throughout his career. From his home base in Baton Rouge, he has photographed chemical plants along the Gulf Coast, the gardens and sacred places of Louisiana, the wildlife sanctuary of Avery Island (home of Tabasco sauce)—all with an awareness of how those subjects mesh with the social issues of his lifetime. His project and 2001 book, *Gettysburg to Vicksburg: The Five Original Civil War Battlefield Parks*, has the widest geographic scope and perhaps the most haunting under-tones of his work to date.

The old trees and somber light in this photograph lend resonance to the Union cemetery at Shiloh Battlefield, where row upon row of stone markers commemorate soldiers who fell in the battle of April 6–7, 1862. Shiloh was the bloodiest Civil War battle up to that time, with nearly 24,000 Union and Confederate casualties. General Ulysses S. Grant, who commanded the Union forces, later wrote that he "saw an open field … so covered with dead that it would have been possible to walk across the clearing, in any direction, stepping on dead bodies, without a foot touching the ground."[*] The grim harvest was only half that of Gettysburg a year later.

EP

---

[*] Ulysses S. Grant, *The Personal Memoirs of Ulysses S. Grant*, vol. 1 (New York: Charles L. Webster and Company, 1885), chapter 25, https://www.gutenberg.org/files/4367/4367-h/4367-h.htm#ch25.

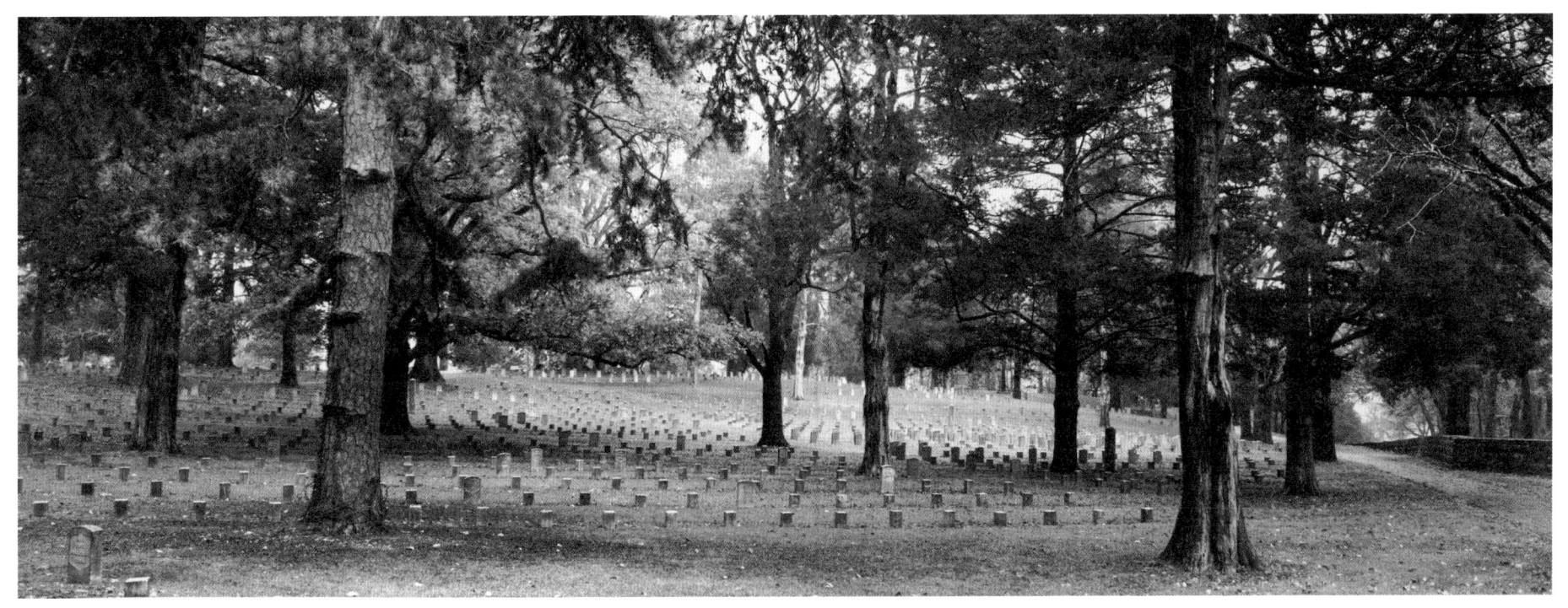

A. J. Meek
American, born 1941
Union Cemetery, Shiloh Battlefield
1994
Gelatin silver print
7 × 19 in. (17.8 × 48.3 cm)
2018.507

Richard Benson was a master printer who perfected many now-common techniques—and some truly unusual methods—for reproducing photographic images in ink on paper. In 1981, he was commissioned to print *Photographs from the Gilman Paper Company Collection*, a remarkable book that stands as the highest achievement in offset reproduction in the predigital age. Together with his other accomplishments, that book earned Benson a MacArthur Foundation "genius" grant in 1986. Benson met Robert Adams on a press check in September 1980, when the pair supervised the printing of Adams's *From the Missouri West* (1980).

Benson's interest in public monuments probably was absorbed from his father, John, a respected stonecutter and designer who ran Rhode Island's John Stevens Shop, a stone-cutting business that has been in continuous operation since 1705. Egalitarian by nature and upbringing, Benson paid honor to the Augustus Saint-Gaudens memorial to Robert Gould Shaw and the 54th Massachusetts Regiment on Boston Common, which memorialized the Black soldiers who fought for the Union, in the first book of his own photographs, *Lay This Laurel* (1973). Small wonder, then, that he gravitated to this monument to Henry Ward Beecher, an ardent abolitionist, a resolute supporter of women's suffrage, and an early Christian adopter of Charles Darwin's theory of evolution.

Benson's photograph omits the figure of Beecher almost entirely. Instead, it focuses on the relationship between the sculpted figures clustered around the base of the statue and the living Black man sleeping on the monument's plinth. The man's limbs join in the rhythm of sculptural gestures; the folds in his coat correspond to the carved drapery of the monument. Even so, the evidently homeless man contrasts with the carefree, aspirational figures above him. The Johnson Street sign in the left background adds a layer of complexity to the picture by evoking President Lyndon B. Johnson, who signed into law the Civil Rights Acts of 1964 and 1968.

EP

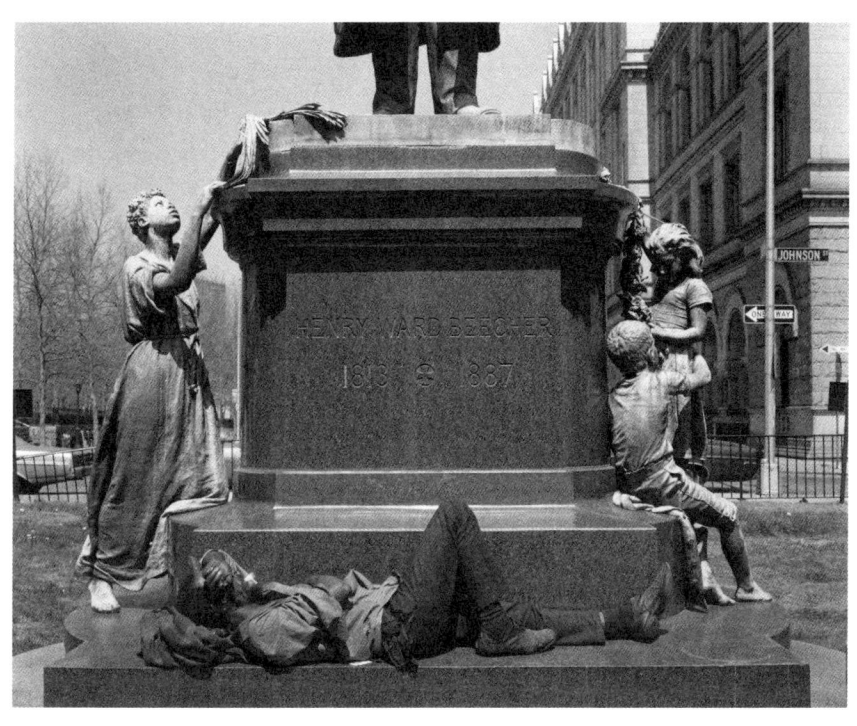

Richard Benson
American, 1943–2017
Henry Ward Beecher Monument, Brooklyn
1974
Inkjet print
13⅝ × 17¼ in. (34.6 × 43.8 cm)
2018.446

Carl Van Vechten worked for newspapers in Chicago, as a critic of music and modern dance for the *New York Times*, and published essays and books of his own before turning to photography in the 1930s. He spent time in Harlem and was a supporter of the arts and ideas of the Harlem Renaissance. As a photographer, Van Vechten focused on making portraits of friends and acquaintances, including dancers, musicians, artists, critics, activists, and writers, among others; between the 1930s and 1960s, he photographed hundreds of the era's cultural figures. He would usually give a print to his sitters but did not make these photographs to sell, and they were exhibited only a few times during his lifetime. In 1941, Van Vechten established the James Weldon Johnson Memorial Collection at the Beinecke Rare Book & Manuscript Library, which houses his photographic negatives and thousands of prints as well as books, documents, and objects from his personal collection and has grown to become an important archive of African American history and culture.

This sensitive portrait of jazz singer Maxine Sullivan is typical of Van Vechten's portrait style: posed in a three-quarter view in front of a boldly pattered fabric background, looking pensively out of the frame. This is one of a series of pictures Van Vechten made of the thirty-year-old singer in his New York City studio on October 7, 1941.

Sullivan came to New York from Pittsburgh in 1937 and started performing in swing clubs along 52nd Street. That same year she got her big break with one of her first recordings, a swing version of the classic Scottish folk song "Loch Lomond." Quickly following that success, she appeared in two Hollywood film musicals and a Broadway show. At the time this photo was made, Sullivan cohosted a live, nationwide, weekly radio show called *Flow Gently, Sweet Rhythm* (1940–41) on Sunday afternoons for CBS with fellow musician, and her then-husband, John Kirby, during which they and other jazz musicians performed music. They were among the first Black musicians to host a nationwide radio show.

KR

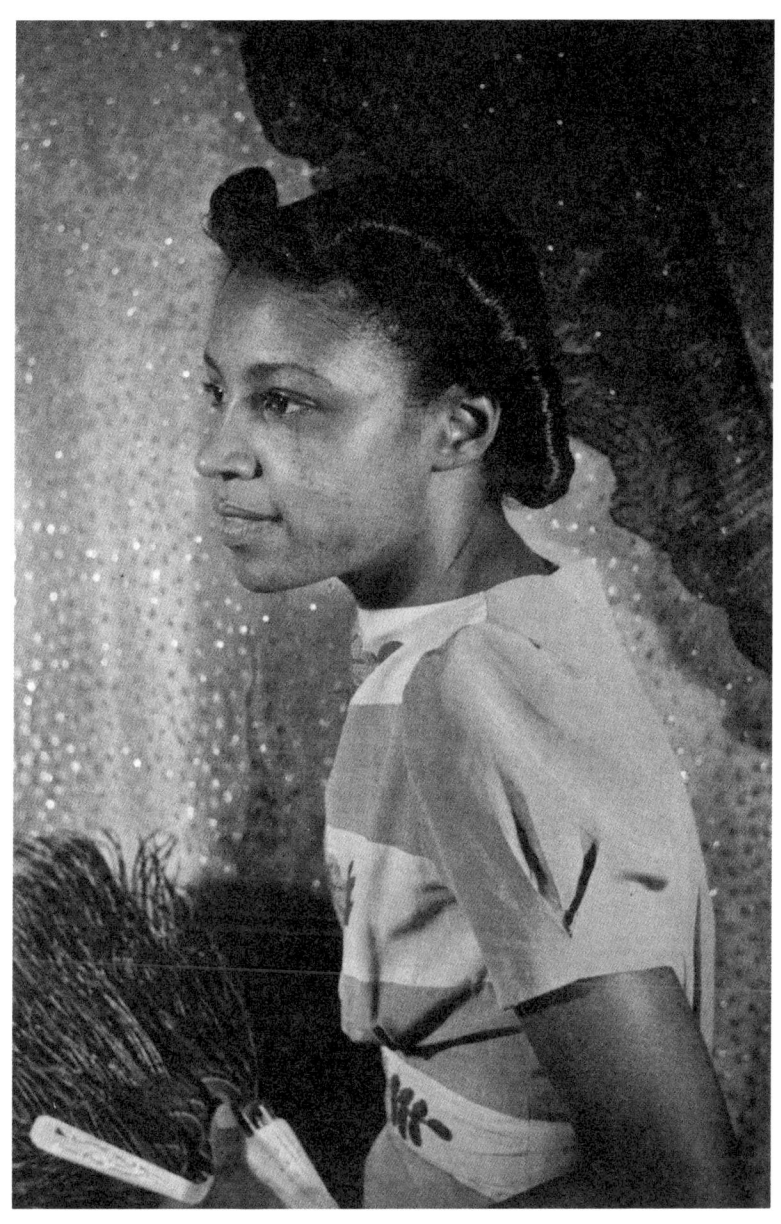

Carl Van Vechten
American, 1880–1964
Maxine Sullivan
1941
Photogravure
8⅞ × 6 in. (22.5 × 15.2 cm)
2018.552

Paul Strand lived in Mexico from 1932 to 1935, having moved there at the invitation of the composer Carlos Chávez to make a documentary film about the fishing community of Alvarado in collaboration with Chávez's nephew, Antonio. They ultimately produced a dramatic feature film about labor rights. *Redes*, directed by Emilio Gómez Muriel and Fred Zinnemann and with a musical score by Silvestre Revueltas, was released in Mexico in 1936 and in France and the United States (as *The Wave*) a year later.

The still photographs Strand made as research for the film signaled his return from abstract formalism to the kind of documentary photographs that he, a one-time acolyte of the photographer and reformer Lewis Hine, had made of New York's urban poor between 1911 and 1916. In Mexico, he concentrated on portraits of laborers and *campesinos* whose livelihoods depended on the land and sea; landscapes and pictures of churches as well as religious artifacts and works of folk art helped to describe the physical and spiritual surroundings in which his portrait subjects lived.

Woman and Basket, Pátzcuaro, Mexico is an important transitional photograph—part character study or portrait and part abstract composition of patterns and forms. The wall and doorway behind the seated woman create a flat field of tone that recalls Constructivist paintings and the taut compositions of painter Piet Mondrian. The shapes and patterns in the woman's clothing and basket, the folds of fabric that sweep across her neck and arms, and the lines where light and dark tones meet—these recall the surprising interlocking forms of Strand's abstract photography. As entrancing as those elements are, however, we return to look at the woman herself: her posture, the glimpse of forearm above her knee, and of course her face. Patient and watchful, she scowls slightly as she seems to listen to a conversation or to eye someone off-camera to her left. Strand may have made the picture to record a type, but he saw an individual and memorialized her on film.

EP

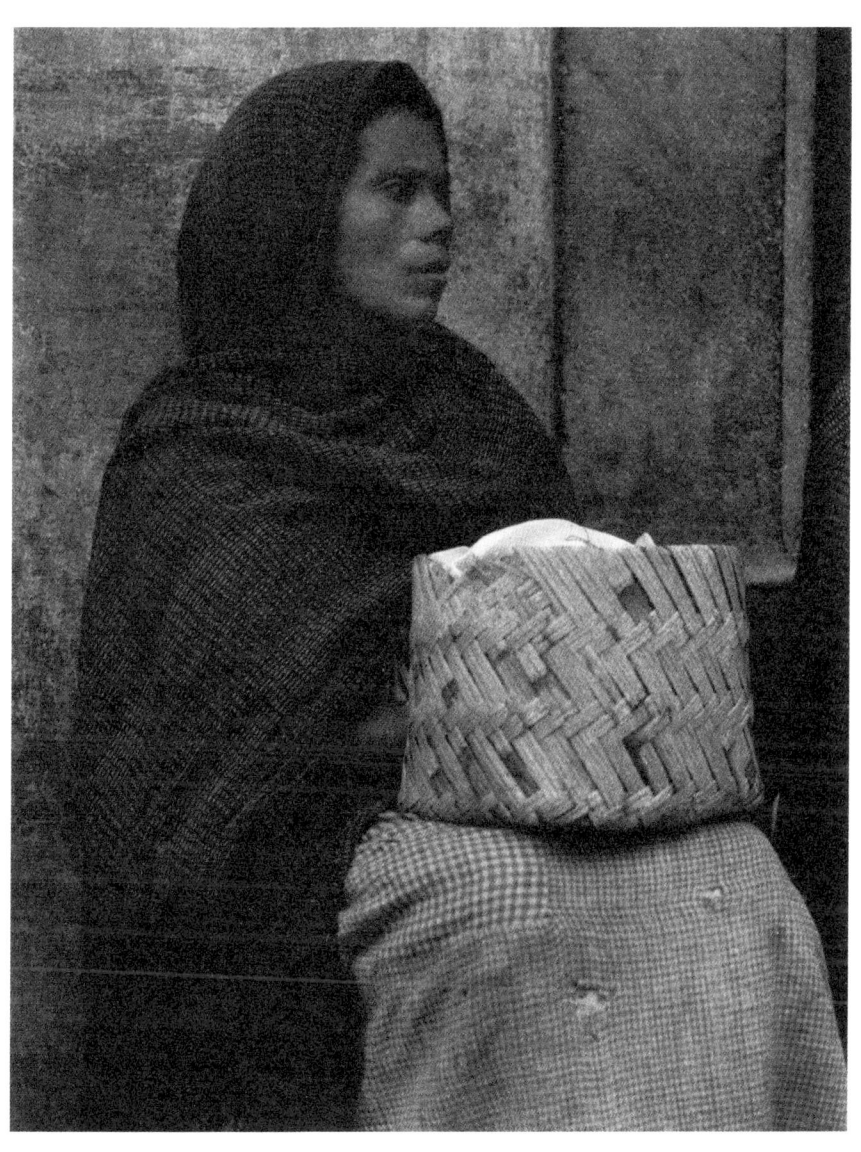

Paul Strand
American, 1890–1976
Woman and Basket, Pátzcuaro, Mexico
1933
Photogravure
6⅜ × 5 in. (16.2 × 12.7 cm)
2018.532

Anthony Hernandez uses careful observation and an openness to serendipitous moments to create his pictures. He began his career making street photographs—walking, observing, recognizing, and quickly capturing picture-worthy moments before the opportunity passed. In an early series called *Public Transit Areas* (1979–80), Hernandez made pictures of people waiting at bus stops all around Los Angeles, where he was born and raised. In each photograph, the specific people, the details of the surroundings, and the interaction between the two are always different, but the pictures all seem to touch on the idea of many private stories coexisting in public space.

Years later, that series influenced a new project titled *Screened Pictures*. For this series, Hernandez set up his camera at bus stop shelters around Los Angeles, many of which were built with perforated metal screen panels. He made pictures of people, trees, and the urban environment around the stops through the "filter" of the metal screen. For *Screened Pictures* #2, Hernandez set up his camera inside a bus stop shelter and captured this image just as the man on the other side stepped into the frame.

The screen is a tool through which Hernandez can see the world differently and explore photography in a new way. By putting the screen in focus, Hernandez emphasizes the forms and colors of the scene within the frame instead of specific details like the man's facial features, his garments, or what he is holding in his hands. The optical experience of viewing a picture like this alters depending on one's proximity: up close, the structure of the screen is more visible, and further back, the view beyond it becomes clearer.

KR

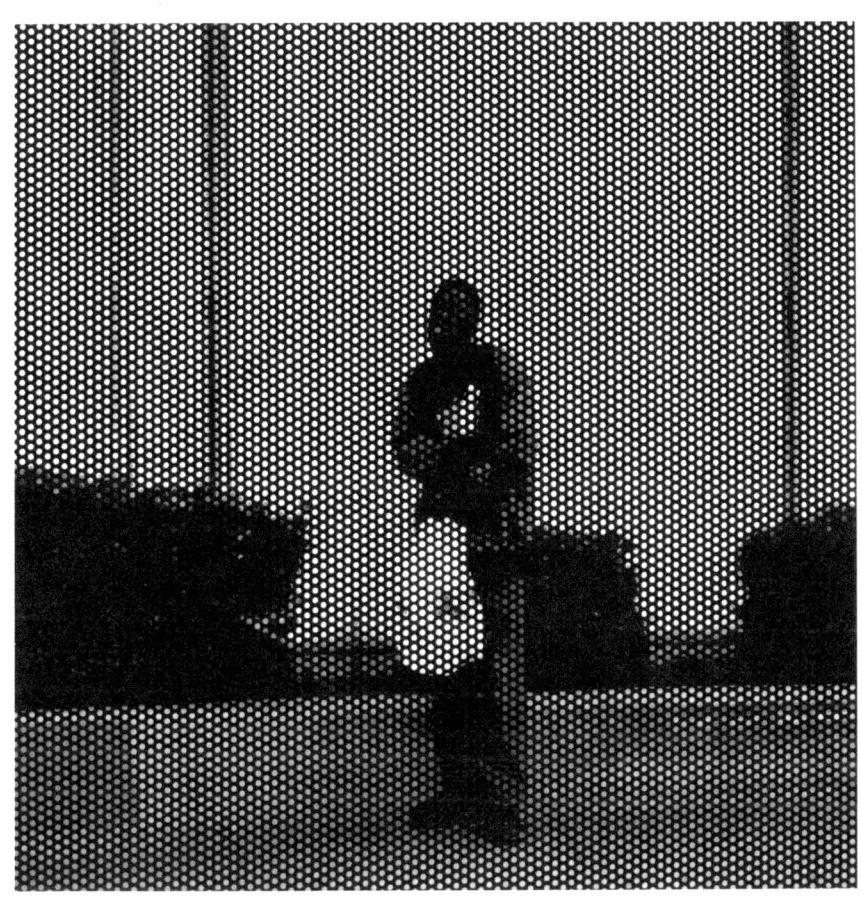

Anthony Hernandez
American, born 1947
Screened Pictures #2
2017
Inkjet print
7½ × 7½ in. (19.1 × 19.1 cm)
2018.478

Jerry Thompson studied photography with Walker Evans at Yale in the 1970s and taught photography there until 1980. His close friendship with Evans gave him unique perspective on the life and ideas of the twentieth-century master photographer, which animates his memoir, *The Last Years of Walker Evans* (1997) and the more recent festschrift *Walker Evans: Depth of Field* (2015). For forty years, Thompson has made his living photographing sculpture for leading museums and collectors in North America and Europe. He also is a widely published portrait photographer.

Today, Lincoln Kirstein is best known as an impresario and as the cofounder, with George Balanchine, of the New York City Ballet in 1948. An energetic writer and editor, he founded the literary and arts magazine *Hound and Horn* with his friend Varian Fry when both men were undergraduates at Harvard. Kirstein wrote one novel, several plays, and at least two volumes of poetry. His essays on the photographers Walker Evans, Henri Cartier-Bresson, W. Eugene Smith, and Richard Benson continue to illuminate the work and ideas of those artists, and his many books and articles on dance express both his fascination with, and his understanding of, creative movement.

Thompson's portrait conveys Kirstein's intensity and seriousness. It gives a sense of the energy and focus he brought to his many endeavors and shows us a man who, at seventy-nine years, felt no inclination to rest on his laurels but who had every intention to keep writing and producing until the end.

EP

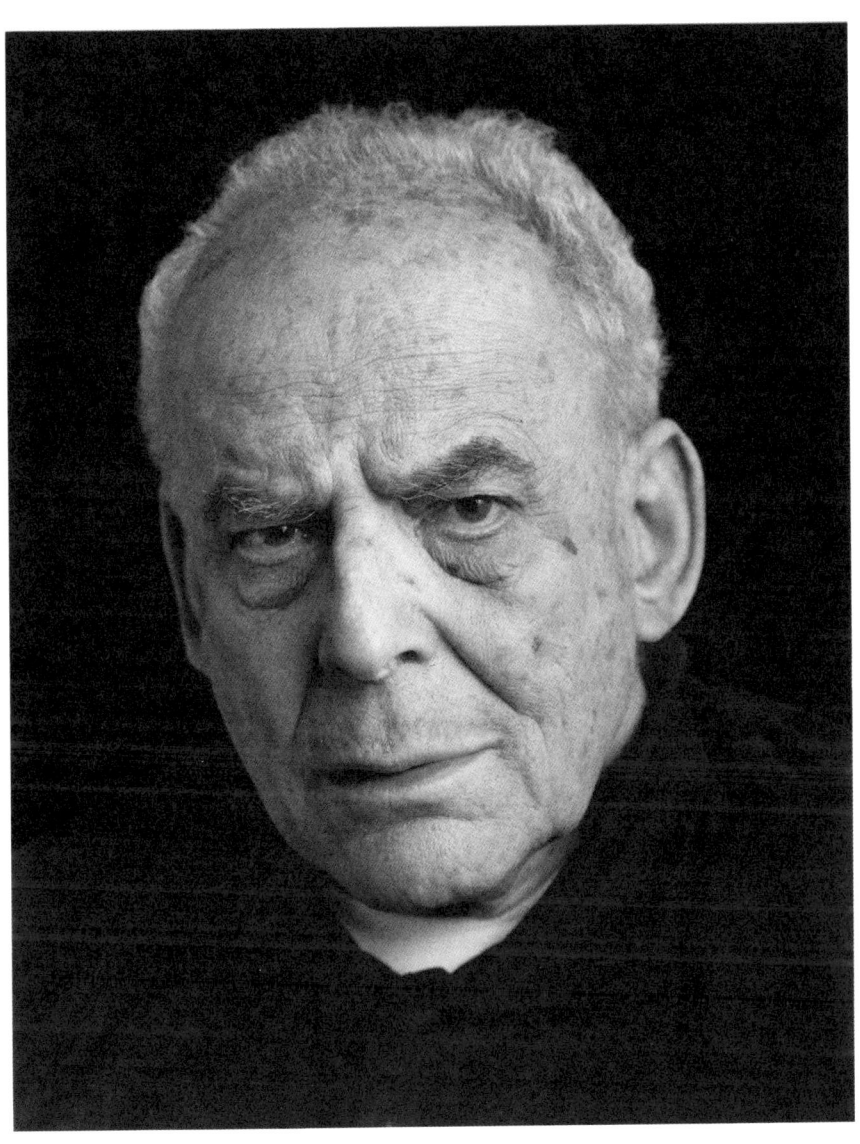

Jerry L. Thompson
American, born 1945
Lincoln Kirstein
1986
Gelatin silver print
9¼ × 7⅜ in. (23.5 × 18.7 cm)
2018.537

When Afonso Malato de Sousa visited us in Longmont, he identified himself as a nonprofessional photographer, saying he earned his living as a computer consultant. The pictures he brought with him reminded me, however, that the history of photography is rich with the achievements of so-called amateurs.

The portrait of French photographer Robert Doisneau, which resulted not only from a fortunate encounter but from quick, educated, and intuitive understanding, is memorable in part because it so exactly matches the respect and affection that is evident in Doisneau's own photography. Few people want their pictures taken without preparations, especially photographers—they know what can happen—and at first Doisneau hesitated but then, probably sensing Afonso's good heart, said "just one," a limitation, but sometimes a help.

Doisneau might have remembered what he had written two years earlier in a preface to a book surveying his work. He liked to think, he said, "of all those seeds gleaned by chance" from street photography, seeds "which perhaps will flower in the hearts of new friends."*

Robert Adams

* Peter Hamilton, *Robert Doisneau: Retrospective* (London: Tauris Parke Books, 1992), 8.

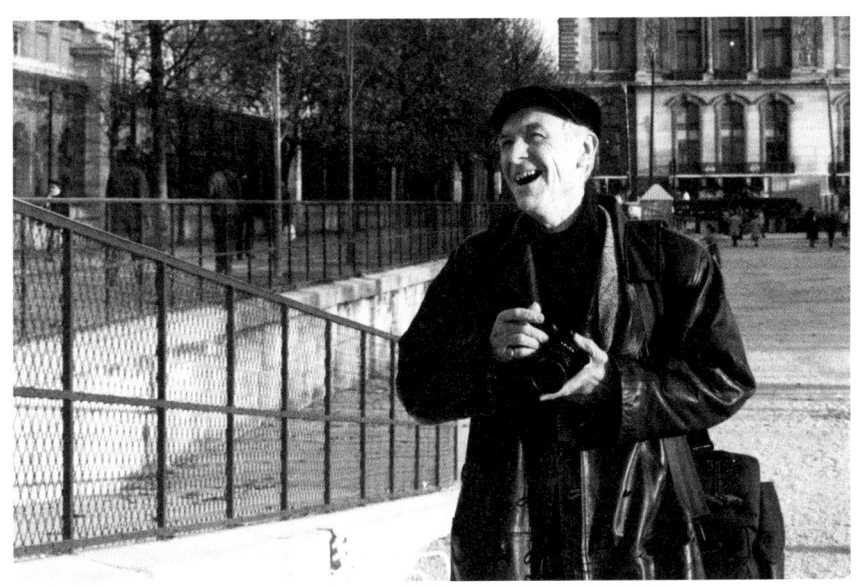

Afonso Malato de Sousa
Portuguese, born 1946
Robert Doisneau
1991
Gelatin silver print
5½ × 8⅜ in. (14 × 21.3 cm)
2018.465

Leo Rubinfien is a photographer, essayist, and critic based in New York City. Early in September 2001, he moved with his wife and small children to an apartment only two blocks from the World Trade Center. A week later, they witnessed the violence of the 9/11 attacks and fled with thousands of others. When they finally were able to return home, they found unimaginable devastation and heartbreak in their home and across the city.

Rubinfien believed that, as damaged as the city was, the attacks focused the world on the struggles for economic, political, and religious dominance that have persisted for decades, if not centuries, and have inflicted deep, seemingly incurable emotional wounds on people around the globe. In 2002, he began to travel and photograph in other cities, searching the faces of ordinary people for signs of the psychic wounds of terrorism and ethnic hatred. After working in streets and public places on six continents, Rubinfien edited his photographs and published them together with his memoir of the attacks and their aftermath in *Wounded Cities* (2008).

Buenos Aires puts us face to face with a man whose gaze into the distance and creased brow convey worry and the slow recognition of whatever he sees over the photographer's shoulder. The camera's shallow depth of field snaps the man's face into crisp focus while everything behind him is blurry, washed out, and off-kilter. In the wounded city of Rubinfien's vision, the man looks watchful and concerned. The photograph is a kind of fiction, of course—the man could be trying to remember the name of the person coming toward him on the sidewalk. Even so, in believing Rubinfein's version we sense the suspicion and fear that terrorism engenders in those who witness its violence.

EP

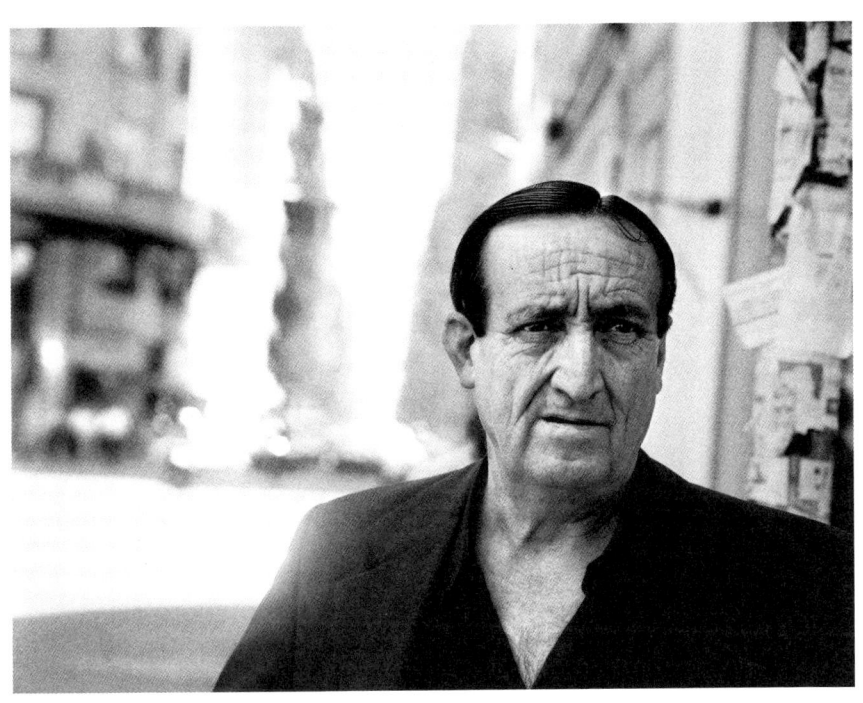

Leo Rubinfien
American, born 1953
Buenos Aires
2006
Inkjet print
8¼ × 10 in. (21 × 25.4 cm)
2018.522

Jack Lueders-Booth entered the vast garbage dump of Tijuana in the 1980s, introduced to its community of garbage pickers by a minister named Pastor Von who had worked there for years. He discovered a world where people work, eat, sleep, and dream amid the refuse of Tijuana's burgeoning population. The pickers sensed that Lueders-Booth was neither a voyeur nor a muckraking journalist looking for a short-lived thrill but a curious and open-hearted man who sought to understand and document what he was seeing. As his collaborator and guide, the writer Luis Alberto Urrea wrote, "They welcomed him in their kitchens and bedrooms, their churches and their bathrooms. They cooked meals for him scrounged out of the dumps." * So began the exploration of human tenacity, ingenuity, and dignity that forms Lueders-Booth's remarkable 2005 book, *Inherit the Land*.

A self-taught photographer, Lueders-Booth traded a career in business for photography at the age of thirty-five and went on to teach photography at Harvard for twenty-nine years. He devoted the better part of his free time and attention during those years to photographing the Tijuana dump and continued the effort through later teaching appointments at Massachusetts College of Art and Design and Rhode Island School of Design. Such long attention to a subject is a rare thing in today's world—he must now be visiting and photographing the grandchildren and great-grandchildren of the people who welcomed him forty years ago. Yet such long-held passion and ever-deeper understanding lend unparalleled gravitas to his work.

Here we see a young woman who has found an exuberant floral-print dress, white stockings, and shiny new shoes in the junk pile. She holds a brush in one hand as she closes her eyes and pulls a white hair band over her forehead. Her surroundings stand in grim contrast to the freshness of her costume, but the picture reminds us of the universal need to step out of one's everyday life and live a little when one can.

EP

* Jack Lueders-Booth and Luis Alberto Urrea, with an afterword by Frank Gohlke, *Inherit the Land* (Boston: Pond Press, 2005), ix.

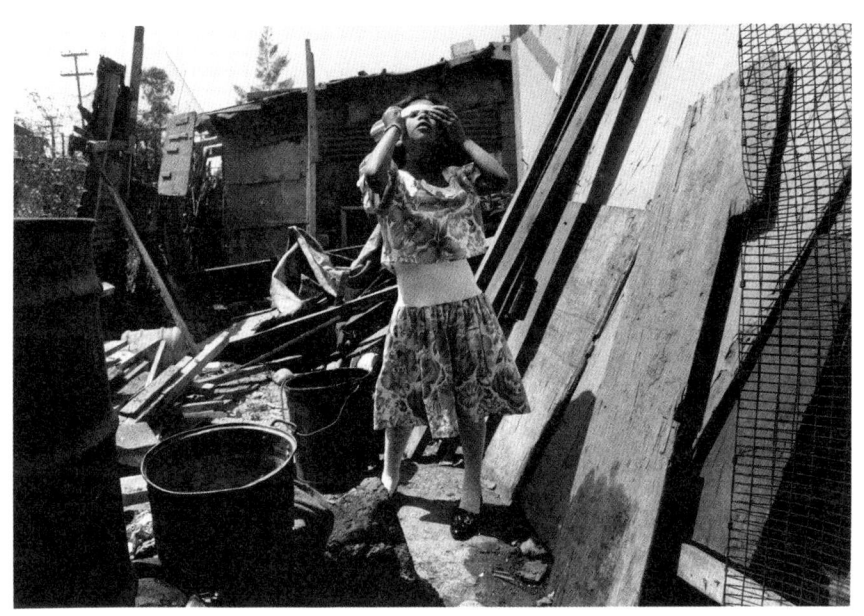

Jack Lueders-Booth
American, born 1935
Untitled, from the series *Inherit the Land*
1990–95
Gelatin silver print
12⅛ × 17⅞ in. (30.8 × 45.4 cm)
2018.505

Judith Joy Ross is best known for her sensitive portraits of people, ranging from children in parks and classrooms to war protesters and politicians. Often driven by empathy or the desire to understand, Ross creates an opportunity for the individual (or group) she is photographing to share something of themselves—for her, the portraits are a collaboration. Ross's pictures, a product of her artistic vision and the openness and trust between her and her subjects, begin to reveal how each person is unique and complex but also connected in their humanity.

Over the course of three years, Ross created a series of pictures of children and teachers at Hazelton public schools in Pennsylvania, which she and other members of her family attended many years before. Her own memories of being a student in the same halls were certainly swirling in her mind as she was making these pictures and, as a result, allowed her to more immediately identify with the people she photographed.

This playful picture of childhood classroom antics is one many can relate to in some way, as either a participant or a witness. The central characters capture our attention first, but the girls in the foreground and the boys in the background to the left show the variety of personalities in every classroom. These photographs evoke a sense of nostalgia about childhood and the possibilities the next generation holds for the future. The moments Ross captures in the lives of these children spark reflection upon our own childhoods and remind us that looking back on the joys and challenges of youth can often reveal a different perspective than the ones we had as children.

KR

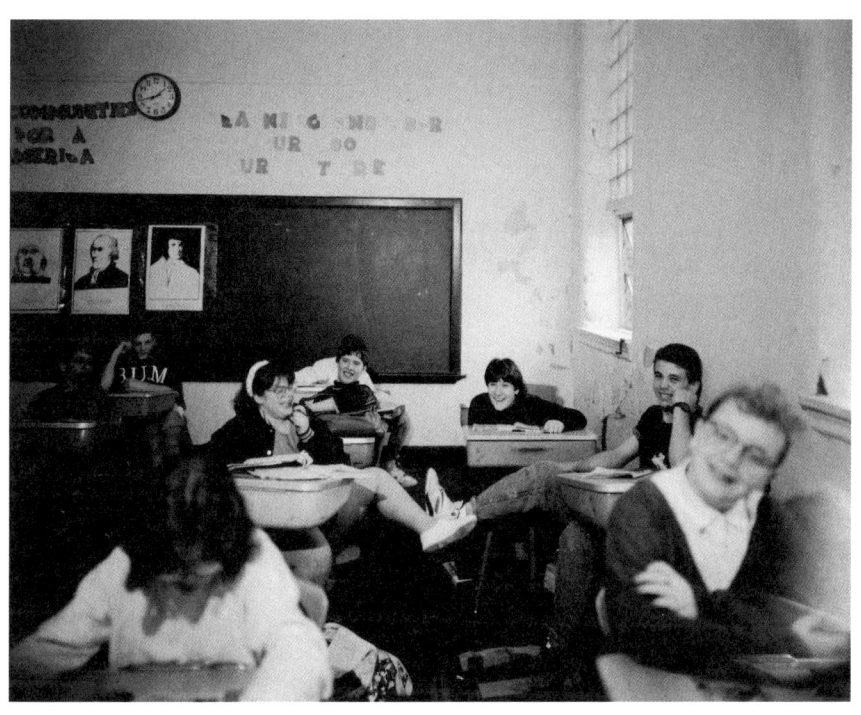

Judith Joy Ross
American, born 1946
Victoria Sherock and Friends Fooling Around, H. F.
Grebey Junior High School, Hazelton, Pennsylvania
1992
Toned gelatin silver printing-out-paper print
8 × 10 in. (20.3 × 25.4 cm)
2018.485

For his well-known *Brown Sisters* series, Nicholas Nixon has photographed his wife and her three sisters, lined up in the same order, every year since 1975. The now forty-six images are a fascinating study of aging and how the vicissitudes of life shape the way people look. It also is a subtle narrative of shifting relationships within the group of siblings: a hand on a shoulder, a turned head, or a momentary glance can suggest feelings of closeness or antipathy that could have been building for a year—but might have started at breakfast that morning.

Nixon reached the public eye in 1975, when his cityscapes of downtown Boston appeared in a landmark exhibition, *New Topographics: Photographs of a Man-Altered Landscape*, at the George Eastman House. Although he returns occasionally to architectural subjects, photographs of people have commanded Nixon's attention since the late 1970s. His photographs of people at leisure on their stoops, of a patient dying from AIDS and his family, and of adults with severe disabilities invite us to look carefully at, and feel empathy for, people we might never see otherwise. A similar blend of tenderness and detachment runs through Nixon's photographs of his family members.

Here, Nixon's son and the family airedale terrier perch inside a window. The boy, with his wide suspenders and rumpled shirt, reaches towards the glass, while the dog looks down at something just below the window. A fresh take on the theme of boy-and-dog companionship, the photograph is also amusing: as Robert Adams pointed out, the creature on the right looks like "a friend in a dog suit." *

EP

---

* Robert Adams, inscription on back of photograph.

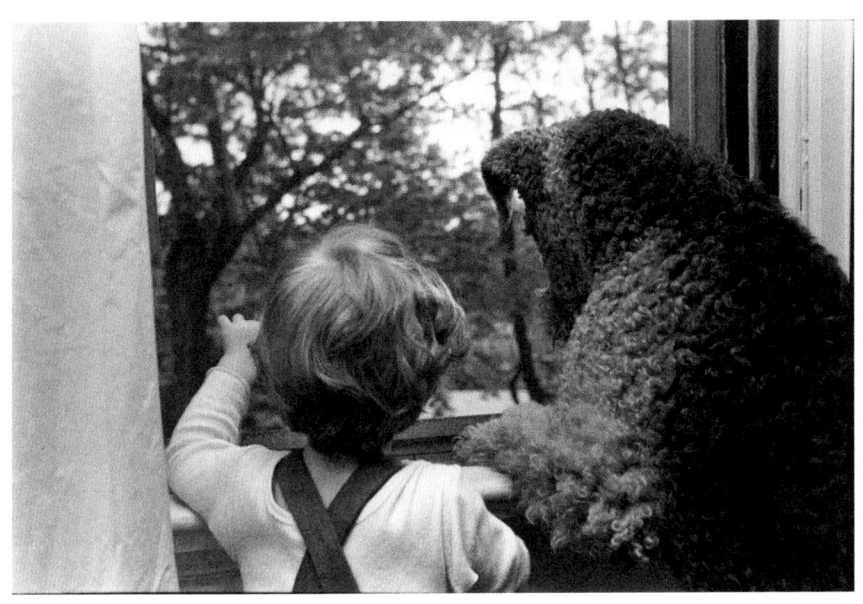

Nicholas Nixon
American, born 1947
Sam and Rufus, Cambridge
1988
Gelatin silver print
4¼ × 6⅜ in. (10.8 × 16.2 cm)
2018.508

L andscape photographers are, on some level, explorers. Whether they travel to the ends of the earth or only to the backyard, they set out to discover and understand something of the world and of themselves. They do not necessarily know what it is they seek, and there is no guarantee they will find it—or recognize it when they do. Theirs is an adventure that relies on the hope that somewhere along the way there will be clarity: a moment when all the parts of a picture coalesce into a meaningful or revelatory whole.

Stuart Klipper has traveled to more far-flung destinations than most fine art photographers. He has photographed extensively on every continent and in all fifty of the United States. After working in Iceland, Greenland, and Svalbard, in 1987 he joined the crew of the sailing ship *Warbaby* on a journey from Argentina to the Antarctic Peninsula and back. Klipper's photographs of extreme latitudes attracted the National Science Foundation's Antarctic Artists and Writers Program, which invited him to photograph and travel with scientists on the continent a record five times. He is one of only a few hundred people who have stood at both the North Pole and the South Pole.

Many photographers work from high vantage points overlooking the sea to study atmospheric effects and reflections from the water. Klipper's photograph, by contrast, puts us right among the heavy swells, where we feel the ocean's weight and its titanic power. The water is churned to froth, wave crests are swept away by the wind, and the horizon seems impossibly far away. The scene is tamed somewhat by beautiful sunlight and clouds overhead.

EP

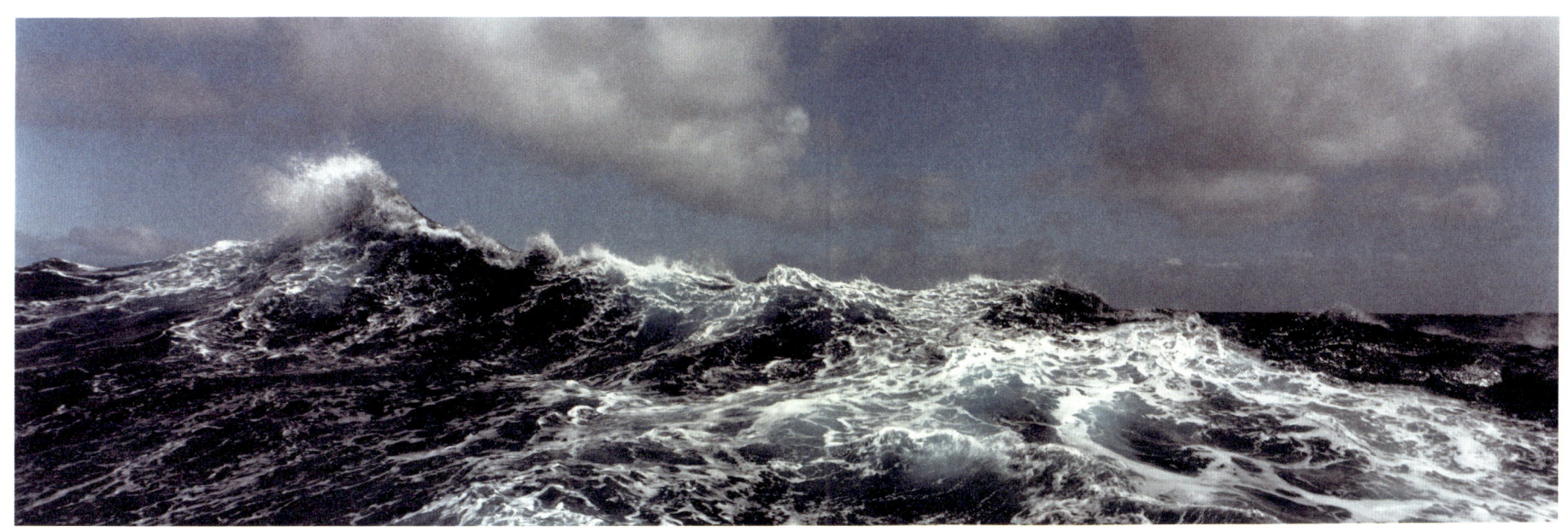

Stuart Klipper
American, born 1941
Swell, Southern Ocean 50˚ S
1992
Chromogenic color print
12 × 38⅛ in. (30.5 × 96.8 cm)
2018.597

Born in Cuba, Peter Henry Emerson trained as a surgeon but gave up his medical career to become England's leading practitioner, publisher, and theorist of photography in a career that stretched from 1885 to the mid-1920s. His 1889 book, *Naturalistic Photography for Students of the Art*, championed a straightforward, narrative approach that was at odds with the studio contrivances of Henry Peach Robinson, Oscar Gustave Rejlander, and others whose work drew inspiration from academic painting.

Emerson directed much of his creative energy toward photographing the people, landscapes, and economies of the fenlands and coastal waters of Norfolk and East Anglia. He viewed that effort, which resulted in half a dozen books in ten years, as an attempt to document and memorialize traditional lifeways that were disappearing. There is a loose connection between Emerson's sympathies and those of Edward S. Curtis, who also used the photogravure process to produce his study of Native Americans some thirty years later. Each photographer's work seems romanticized or nostalgic today, judged by current attitudes and information rather than by those that guided the making of the work.

This photograph shows three men in a small lug-rigged boat as they negotiate a narrow passage in a marsh. There is a small clapboard house on the shore some distance away, surrounded by a stand of trees. A small windmill may have been used to pump water from low ground near the house. The city of Norwich hunkers in the distance—the steeple of St. Peter Mancroft church is just visible through the haze. The water is smooth, the marsh grasses are unruffled, and the men seem to work without haste. Smoke from the house's chimney drifts horizontally, indicating a stiff breeze that the boatmen seem to take in stride, comfortable in their jobs and their environment.

EP

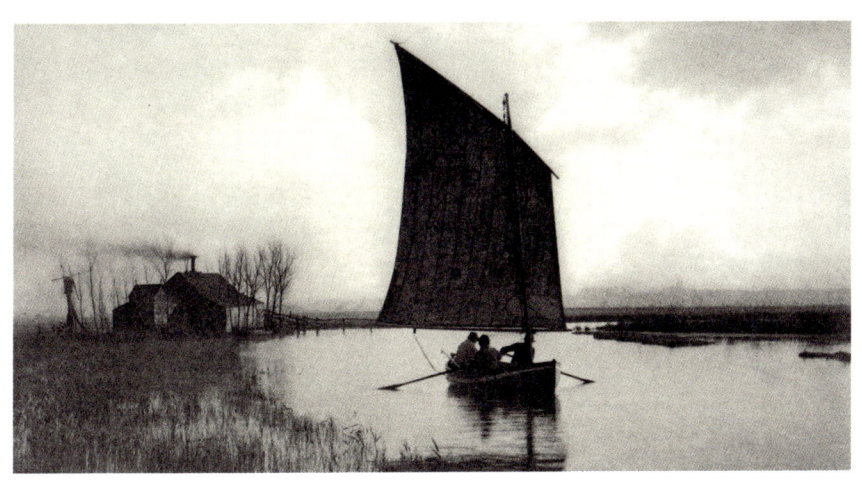

Peter Henry Emerson
British, born in Cuba, 1856–1936
The Old Order and the New
1886
Photogravure
4⅝ × 9 in. (11.8 × 22.9 cm)
2018.466

Alfred Stieglitz was a key photographer and promoter of fine art photography and modernism in the United States in the first half of the 1900s. He was a founding member of the New York Photo-Secession, a fine art photography club; was the editor of their quarterly publication *Camera Work*; and opened and ran three New York galleries: Little Galleries of the Photo-Secession (a.k.a. 291; 1905–17), The Intimate Gallery (1925–29), and An American Place (1929–46).

New York City and its changing form over the first few decades of the twentieth century was the subject of many photographs throughout Stieglitz's career. In the 1930s, Stieglitz made approximately sixty views of the New York City skyline from these windows of his apartment on the thirtieth floor of the Shelton Hotel and his gallery An American Place. The elevated views from these windows inspired photographs of a cityscape shaped by light and shadow.

The silhouettes and cast shadows of buildings anchor this image with solid black forms. A glimpse of a partially illuminated façade abruptly interrupts the darkness with a band of light descending to the bottom right of the frame. This small detail reminds us that the shadowed forms are in fact a mass of buildings in a densely packed city. Stieglitz captured the sunlight as it hit these buildings at different points in the day and seasons. The high contrast between the light and shadows produces a geometric play of forms that Stieglitz framed and called attention to in this image. The fact that he made many photographs from a similar vantage point emphasizes that these pictures are about looking. Stieglitz saw this view from his home on a daily basis, but when looking closely and consistently, he perceived what he was seeing was in fact ever-changing because of the light, the construction of the city, and himself.

KR

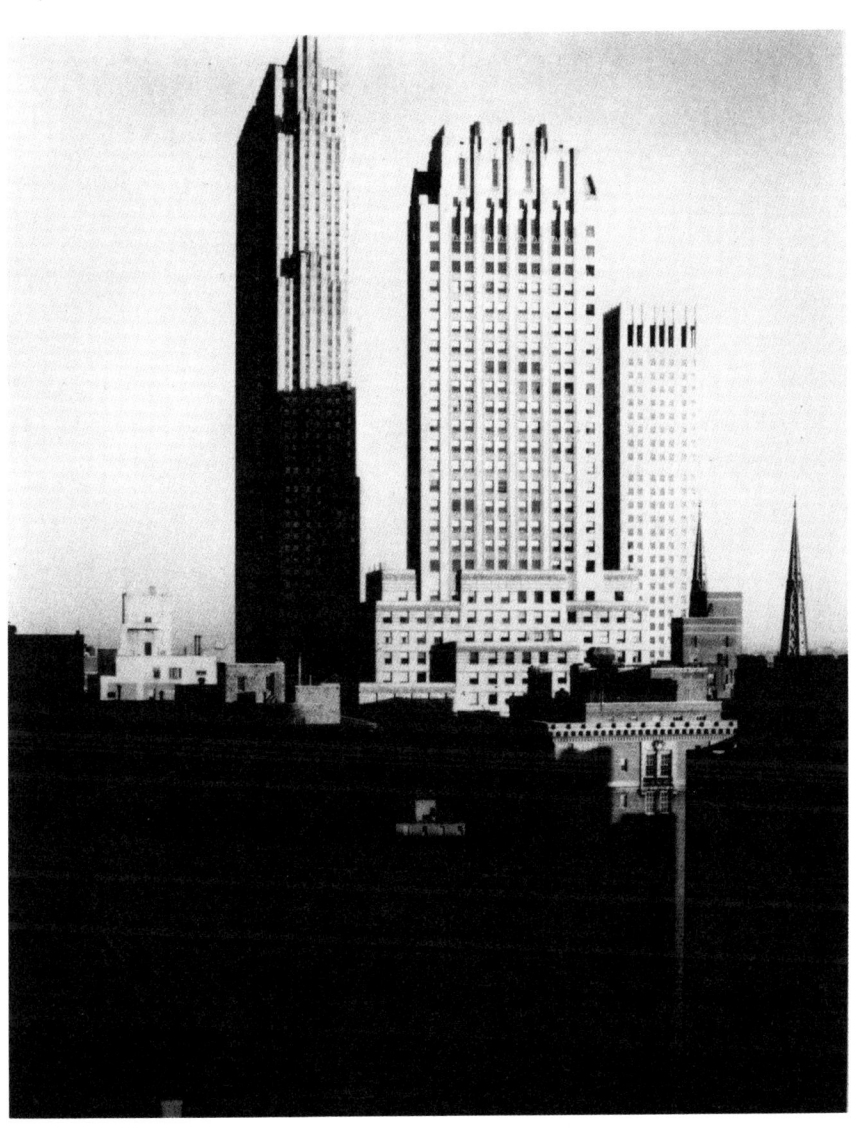

Alfred Stieglitz
American, 1864–1946
New York from the Shelton
1935
Photogravure
9⅝ × 7½ in. (24.5 × 19.1 cm)
2018.534

Dorothy Norman was a photographer, writer, and editor who was involved in social activism throughout her life. Norman and Alfred Stieglitz first met in 1927 when she visited Stieglitz's The Intimate Gallery (1925–29) in New York City and was inspired by the art and people that filled it. The two had a strong connection and would remain close the rest of his life. Norman oversaw operations at Stieglitz's next and last gallery, An American Place (1929–46), and after his death, she published books about his life and work, including *Stieglitz Memorial Portfolio* (1947) and *Alfred Stieglitz: An American Seer* (1973). Norman began pursuing photography herself in 1931 under the mentorship of Stieglitz. She made pictures at An American Place, around New York, Cape Cod, and later India, as well as many portraits of artists and writers.

A portrait can express much more about an individual than simply their likeness. This beautifully composed picture, one of the many Norman made of Stieglitz, communicates a great deal about his life, art, and influence. We see Stieglitz seated at his desk at An American Place, touching up one of the many portraits he made of Norman as light spills in from the window outside the right of the frame. In the background, two John Marin paintings sit on a ledge against the wall— Marin was one of the few artists Stieglitz supported throughout the entirety of his career and showed at all three of his galleries. Paintings by Marin also happened to be on the walls of The Intimate Gallery when Norman and Stieglitz first met. Between the two paintings is one of Stieglitz's own creations, a recent photograph of the New York skyline (p. 61). We see Stieglitz at work in his gallery, surrounded by his art and that of one of the artists he supported, being photographed by a cherished colleague, student, and companion, Dorothy Norman.

KR

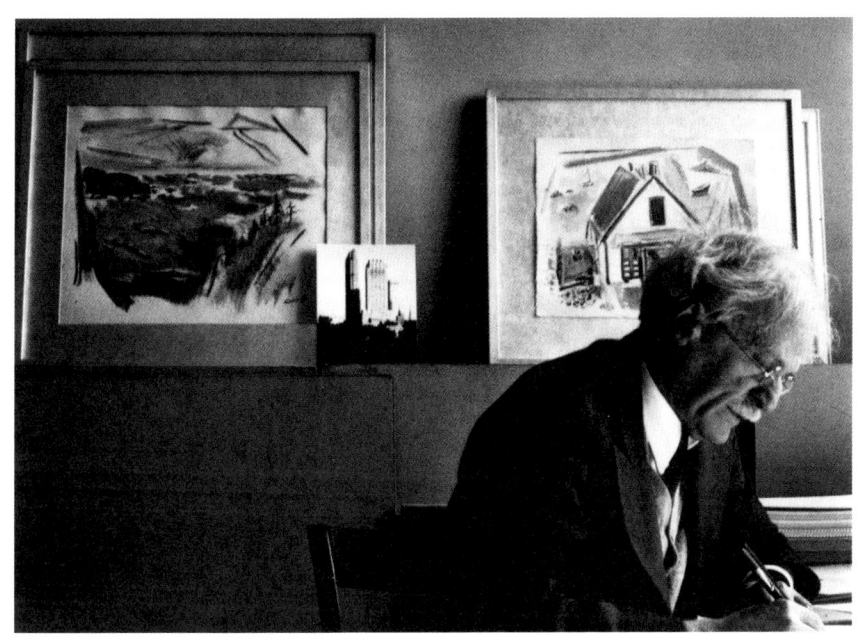

Dorothy Norman
American, 1905–1997
Alfred Stieglitz Spotting Portrait of Dorothy Norman, with Marin Paintings and Stieglitz Photograph in Background, An American Place, New York
1930s
Gelatin silver print
2¾ × 3⅞ in. (7 × 9.8 cm)
2018.567

The history of photography is sparsely populated with artists who carried on protracted love affairs with the cities where they lived and sought to acknowledge every wrinkle of the urban landscapes they knew best. Eugène Atget explored and photographed Paris from the 1890s to his death in 1927. Berenice Abbott, who knew Atget and helped rescue his life's work from oblivion, returned from Paris to New York in 1929 and photographed the city for a decade on her own and as an employee of the Works Project Administration Federal Art Project. Sometimes exuberant, sometimes bittersweet, their pictures tell us what it is to see a familiar place with fresh, loving eyes. Of course, their work also serves to remind us what has been lost to fire, economic change, and the urban planner's pencil.

In *Space and Place: The Perspective of Experience*, geographer Yi-Fu Tuan identified "place" as the location where memory and shared stories of family, community, and personal experience create a sense of belonging.* Bob Thall, like Atget and Abbott, has devoted most of his life and thought to photographing his place: Chicago.

Thall's photographs strike us as authoritative because he knows Chicago so well and has worked there for so long. Yet it is easy to overlook how, for a photographer like him, deciding where and especially *when* to make a picture is an expression of connoisseurship as well as familiarity and skill. If he had made this photo when the sun didn't come streaking along the sidewalk and the police hadn't left their car by the curb, the place would not have held its ramshackle glow. Certainly, that lone man would not have stood on the corner, casting his long shadow and wondering what that man with the camera was doing. The picture is a story of the place told slowly and in every sweet detail.

EP

---

*Yi-Fu Tuan, *Space and Place: The Perspective of Experience* (Minneapolis: University of Minnesota Press, 1976).

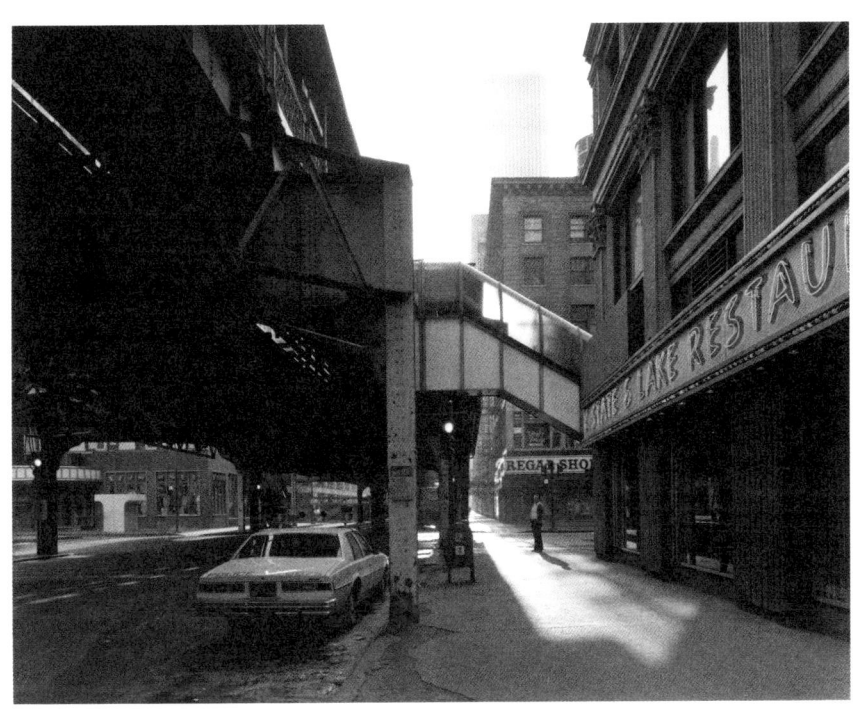

Bob Thall
American, born 1948
Chicago
1981
Gelatin silver print
13½ × 16¾ in. (34.3 × 42.6 cm)
2018.536

Self-taught photographer Mark Cohen was born in Wilkes-Barre, Pennsylvania, and lived there until he was seventy years old. From the 1960s, he was impelled to wander his hometown streets and alleys with a camera and to photograph a seemingly random assortment of strangers, animals, and the rusted or windblown detritus of a declining industrial city. He first came to prominent attention when the Museum of Modern Art presented a solo exhibition of his work in 1973.

Cohen often worked up close to his subjects, using electronic flash or long shutter speeds and sometimes both. That technique and Cohen's acute sense of possibility resulted in pictures that evoke intimacy and emotional distance at the same time. The faces and gritty surfaces convey both weariness and stubborn determination. Cohen shares in his city's malaise and its moments of camaraderie, but he is a detached observer rather than an insider.

At first glance, this appears to be a rather plain photograph of the bald tire and wheel well on a much-used, possibly abandoned, car. The paint is dull from age and rough weather, and the brightwork—hubcap and body side molding—is gone. Oil stains on the pavement hint at leaking fluids no one has bothered to clean up. But the trigger that made Cohen stop in his tracks was not the car but the bright smudge that hovers between his eye and the wheel—a wasp in flight. That stinging insect breathes a whiff of fresh life into its tired surroundings.

EP

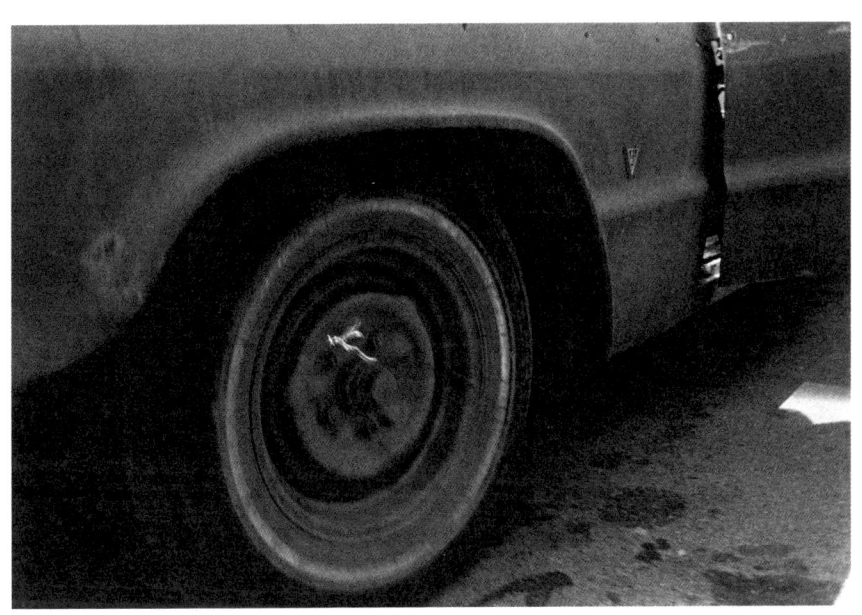

Mark Cohen
American, born 1943
Wasp Over Wheel
1976
Gelatin silver print
12½ × 18½ in. (31.8 × 47 cm)
2018.506

Chuck Forsman is a painter and photographer based in Boulder, Colorado, where he was on the art faculty at the University of Colorado from 1971 to 2008. His best-known paintings address clashes between contemporary American society and the environment and, in some cases, the distance between mainstream values and those of Indigenous peoples. A veteran of the Vietnam War, Forsman has made several trips to Southeast Asia to sketch and photograph, including one when he traveled the length of the Mekong River with one of his daughters. Preparatory works from those journeys inform an ongoing series of large canvases that attempt to square cultural differences, history, and Forsman's feelings about his war experience and America's continuing role in foreign conflicts.

Throughout his career Forsman photographed through the windshield of his car to create studies for paintings. By the 1990s, however, he came to see those photographs as finished artworks in their own right; a short, intense burst of work resulted in his *Western Rider* series, which was published by The Center for American Places in 2003 — the first of four photography books he has created so far. *Western Rider* offers an amalgam of serene vistas, quirky roadside attractions, chance encounters, and adverse weather that is amusing and hallucinatory by turns.

Blizzard, U.S. 287, Southern Wyoming, one of seventy-seven photographs in the *Western Rider* book, will look familiar to any westerner who has driven in a snowstorm with an onslaught of white streaking towards the windshield. The experience pits one's misgivings against one's stubbornness and leads to the realization that one is suddenly and completely alone, even with other people or a dog in the car. In the wider context of Forsman's series, this one reminds us that travel in the West is about much more than sightseeing.

EP

Chuck Forsman
American, born 1944
Blizzard, U.S. 287, Southern Wyoming
1997
Gelatin silver print
6½ × 9¾ in. (16.5 × 24.8 cm)
2018.470

Bill Wylie lived in Fort Collins, Colorado, and taught photography at Colorado State University before he accepted a professorship in the University of Virginia's art department. On summer drives back to Colorado, he photographs the towns and landscapes along his favorite cross-country route, U.S. Route 36, which cuts a nearly straight line from eastern Ohio to Rocky Mountain National Park.

Bird City, Kansas is, in some respects, the twenty-first century echo of the postcard image of Gordon, Nebraska (p. 23), but sleepy silence has replaced the pride and optimism of the earlier picture. The old gas station on the left and the overhead doors on the right suggest that Wylie stood a half a block or so from Bird City's commercial center to make this photograph. Gentle afternoon light washing over the asphalt and broken concrete and illuminating the trees across the highway conveys the wistful beauty of the place. The water tower in the distance, with the town's name on its side, is just high enough to produce good water pressure and tall enough to serve as a beacon to travelers far out on the plains.

Wylie's book *Route 36* can be seen as an homage to the photographs in *Prairie*, a 1978 book by Robert Adams that looked at the landscapes of eastern Colorado with wisdom and affection. At the same time, Wylie's linear progress along the highway recalls his early *Riverwalk* project (published as a book in 2000), for which he walked the 150-mile length of the Cache la Poudre River from its confluence with the South Platte River near Greeley, Colorado, to its headwaters in Rocky Mountain National Park.

EP

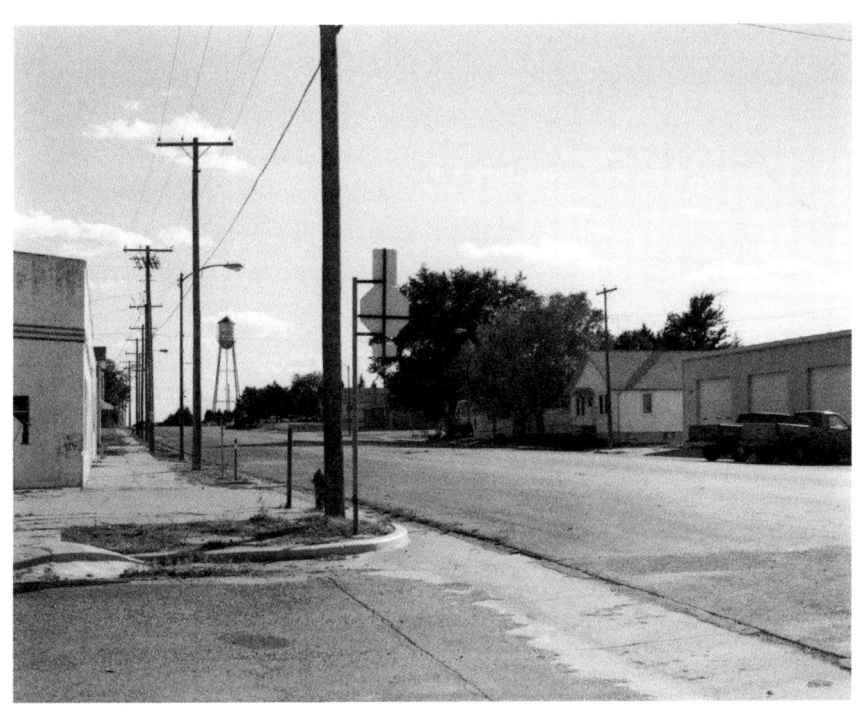

William Wylie
American, born 1957
Bird City, Kansas
2007
Gelatin silver print
7 × 8⅞ in. (17.8 × 22.5 cm)
2018.583

Based in Tucson, Arizona, Daniel Cheek embraces the idea that human-made landscapes express not only the idiosyncratic impulses of individuals but also the broad trends in a society's attitudes toward nature and toward itself. In his view, the parks and natural areas where people go to enjoy nature are modified and controlled for the sake of safety and convenience. Cheek's photographic series entitled *Separation* and *The Mediated Landscape* point to the distance that lies between wilderness and American life and describe how governments and nonprofit organizations create acceptable illusions of wildness.

Cheek uses a large format view camera and prints his pictures so that the film edges show; here, he has joined two separate pictures together to form a panorama. It takes a moment to account for the strong black line where the two images meet—it makes the picture looks like it was taken through the window of a bus—but once we accept it as an artifact of Cheek's process, we can fully enjoy what he shows us.

Driven by curiosity to see the kinds of places where people spend leisure time close to nature, Cheek visited Lake Chabot Regional Park, which lies in the Berkeley Hills about twenty-five miles east of San Francisco, California. Trees surround a grassy slope in the center of the picture and overhang a dirt road as it disappears into shadow on the left. The light, the time of day, and the contour of the land evoke warmth and quiet, as if one were walking alone on a summer afternoon. The photograph reminds us that such modest pleasures often are enough.

EP

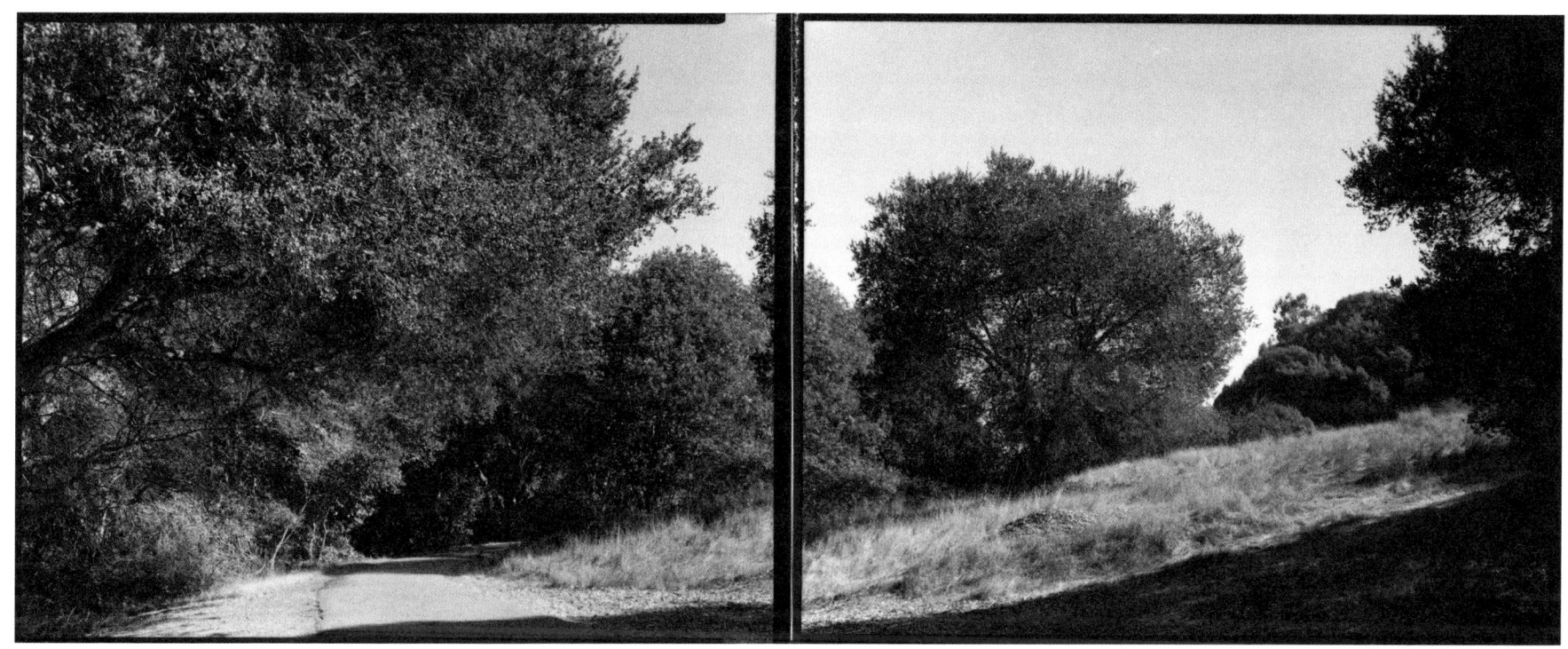

Daniel Cheek
American, born 1978
Lake Chabot Regional Park
2009
Gelatin silver prints
Diptych 8 × 20 in. (20.3 × 50.8 cm)
2018.448A-B

Edward Weston is famous for the formal rigor of his photographs and for his belief that a photograph should reveal, as he wrote in his journal, "the very substance and quintessence of the thing itself." * Which is to say that, for Weston, to make a photograph was to embrace the tangible presence of one's subject without interjecting a secondary meaning or resorting to visual effects. One might reasonably suspect some of Weston's still life photographs of engaging in metaphor, but on the whole, what you see in a Weston photograph is what you get. We value his best work not for its humanitarian insight but for its concentrated looking.

Weston demonstrated his convictions and his expert sense of form in *Eel River Ranch*. He found a vantage point where the gently unfolding landscape was as clear as could be: pools of sunlight wash over the hillsides, fields, and trees in the foreground and delineate each tree on the far hillside. After taking it all in, the eye zigzags from the angled road and fence line at the bottom of the picture to the row of trees that follows a small stream up and to the right, then down through the central grassy field and back up another line of trees, through another field . . . The movement unfolds with perfect ease and continues to the delicate shadows and highlights of thick forest. The picture has a freshness and beauty that proposes that, even if just for a moment, things are right in the world.

EP

* Edward Weston and Beaumont Newhall, eds., *The Daybooks of Edward Weston, vol. 1: Mexico* (New York: Aperture, 1973), 55.

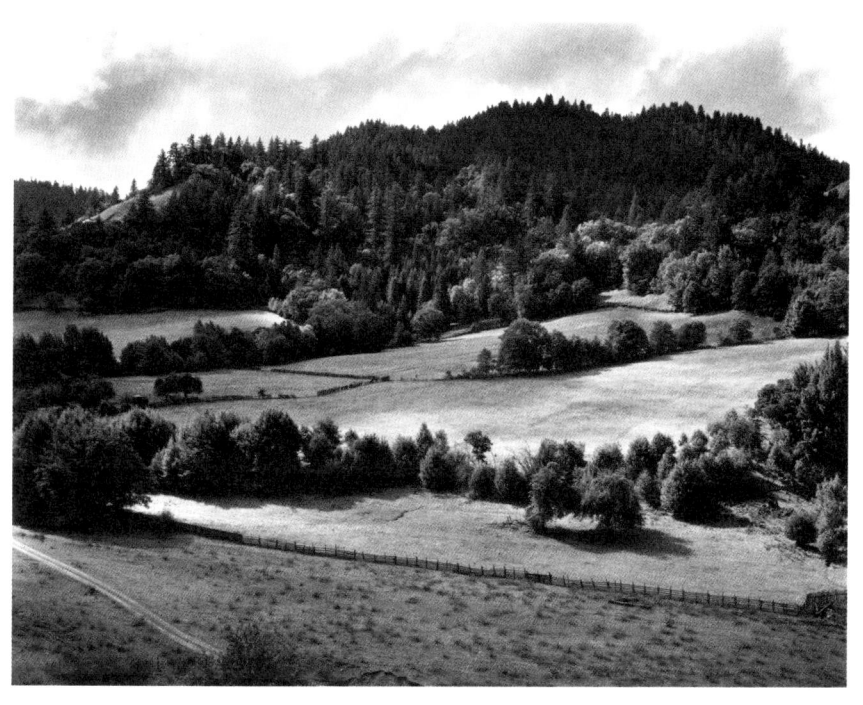

Edward Weston
American, 1886–1958
Eel River Ranch
1937
Gelatin silver print
7⅜ × 9⅜ in. (18.7 × 23.8 cm)
2018.553

Prehistoric Lake Missoula formed in what is now western Montana and northern Idaho some 15,000 years ago, when a lobe of the great Cordilleran Ice Sheet dammed the Clark Fork river. At its peak, the lake contained a volume of water equal to half of Lake Michigan. About forty times in two thousand years, the ice dam gave way and the lake water rushed through eastern Washington state to the Columbia River. Colossal floods of water, ice, and huge rocks swept away more than fifty cubic miles of topsoil and carved deep channels through the wide area now known as the Channeled Scablands.

The subject of this photograph, Moses Coulee, is one of the most impressive of the channels scoured by the Lake Missoula outburst floods. A basalt cliff—the remnant of an ancient lava flow—stands sentinel over an expansive sagebrush flat. Disarmingly simple and rendered in rich brown tones, the photograph could be a product of the nineteenth century but is the fairly recent work of an artist who is still very much alive. It sidesteps easy drama for description so direct one can almost smell the sagebrush and hot stone.

Charles Katz is an attorney and one-time software entrepreneur who has served on the National Council of World Wildlife Fund and as an advisor to various environmental groups at Stanford University. He has published four books of photography devoted to geology and environmental preservation. *Moses Coulee* is from a portfolio of photogravure prints Katz created in support of the Nature Conservancy in Washington.

EP

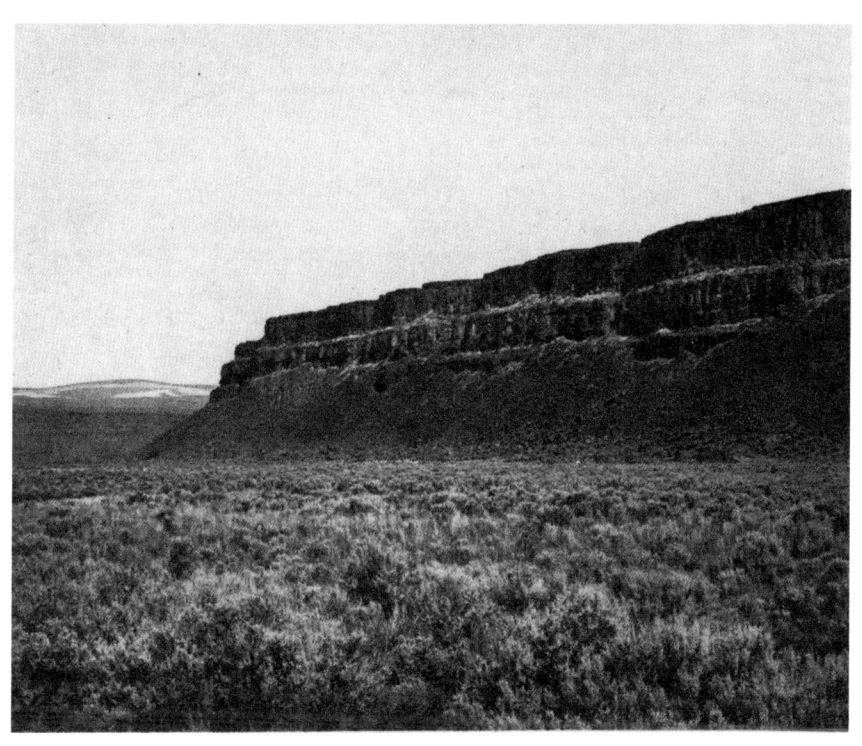

Charles J. Katz Jr.
American, born 1948
Moses Coulee
2004
Photogravure
4⅜ × 5⅜ in. (11.1 × 13.7 cm)
2018.595

Mark Ruwedel has photographed the American and Canadian West for thirty years and has compiled an archive of work that extols both the beauty of the region and our willingness to treat it as an exploitable—even an expendable—resource. More than most photographers of his generation, he responds to the work of those nineteenth-century masters whose images shaped popular perceptions of the West and enlarged its mythical proportions. By thoroughly absorbing the formal and spatial sensibilities of, for example, Timothy O'Sullivan's and Andrew Joseph Russell's work from 150 years ago, Ruwedel has created carefully restrained images of western landscapes; adding together the details of his carefully considered photographs, viewers arrive at a new appreciation of the region's horrors as well as its pleasures.

Ruwedel does not simply mimic the work of his predecessors or follow their footsteps to rephotograph the scenes they witnessed. He is craftier than that, as evidenced in his *Pictures of Hell*—for which he photographed places where the hopelessness, fear, or closed-mindedness of early white settlers inspired them to assign place names that mentioned the devil and his inhospitable domain. The artist's droll humor shows in the undertaking, but his photographs prove how misguided the pioneers were: there is profound beauty in those seemingly godforsaken places. If the perception of beauty is a matter of what one knows and what one is willing to accept, Ruwedel's photographs teach us to love the ragged, empty landscapes of the American desert.

Ruwedel's awareness of his place—both in relation to earlier photogra-phers and as a witness to his own time—adds the weight of historical significance to his work. His knowledge of geology further extends the temporal depth of his work. In this picture, long shadows fall over Death Valley, where Lake Manley formed 185,000 years ago. The lake all but vanished 10,000 years ago, leaving mudflats, salt flats, and the resonant hush that suffuses Ruwedel's picture.

EP

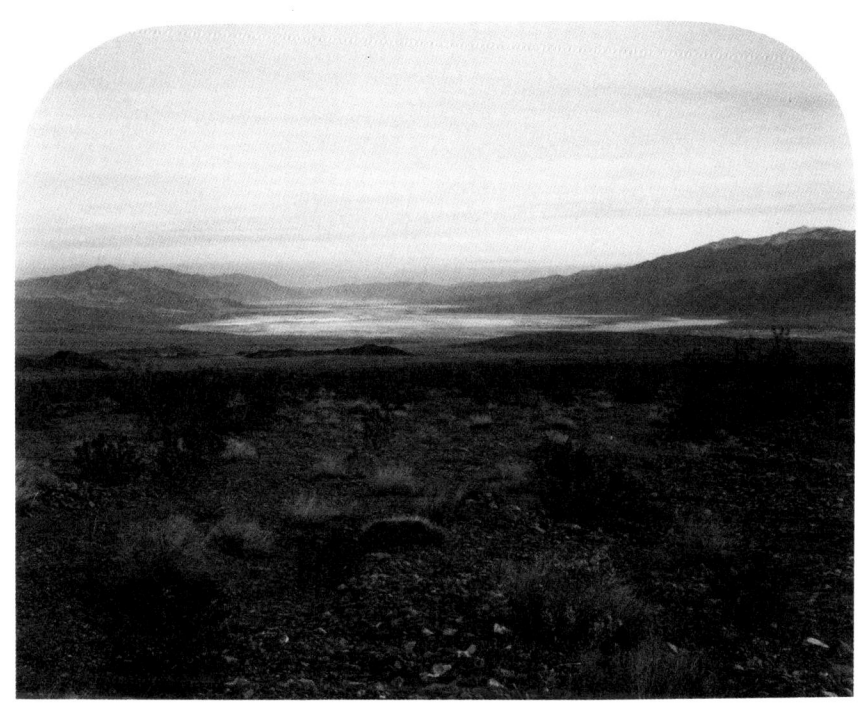

Mark Ruwedel
American, born 1954
Death Valley—A View of Ancient Lake Manly from Hell's Gate
1995
Gelatin silver print
7⅜ × 9⅜ in. (18.7 × 23.8 cm)
2018.529

Bob is and has been for over forty years one of the three or four photographers whose work I love most in all the world. His touch is light, even when his subject is heavy. He is like a sculptor who can tap three chips from a block of stone and devastate you. Bob set out his ambition and its rationale when he said (I'm paraphrasing): "A photograph should look easy to make. Otherwise it conveys a message that beauty is a hard thing to find in the world." Making anything look easy is the hardest thing in the world.

Bob was attracted to pictures of mine that carried a suggestion of something impending. In the seventies and eighties, that something was the threat of nuclear annihilation, but it could be generalized to a reminder that all life takes place alongside the ambiguous comfort of mortality. I don't remember whether he said anything of the sort when he chose this photograph, but it lends itself in part to that reading. A thunderstorm is moving into the frame from the left. Counterposed to the chaotic potency of the coming storm is the vast cornfield, whose regular rows, filling the frame from left to right, recede seemingly to infinity. Temporally we come upon this scene close to the moment when the sun, sinking below the distant edge of the storm, graces the roadside weeds and productive fields alike with the same momentary gilding light.

Why do photographers trade their work with other photographers? In part it's because some pictures stab me in the heart, and the only way to soothe the hurt is to be able to revisit the experience and feel it again, especially in the form that most closely embodies what the artist had in mind. I am fortunate if the maker of the image happens to be a friend who feels a similar attraction to one of my own pictures; over the years Bob and I have enjoyed that ritual on several occasions. I always felt honored and enriched by the exchange, not only because I went home with objects that I knew would give me pleasure for years into the future but because it affirmed the existence of a community of artists that sustains me still, even though we are widely scattered and may be rarely in touch. To know that, no matter how isolated I might feel or actually be, I am engaged in a shared enterprise that is of great consequence for the culture at large (whether they're aware of it or not) is more than ample compensation. Well, that and some truly extraordinary prints.

Frank Gohlke

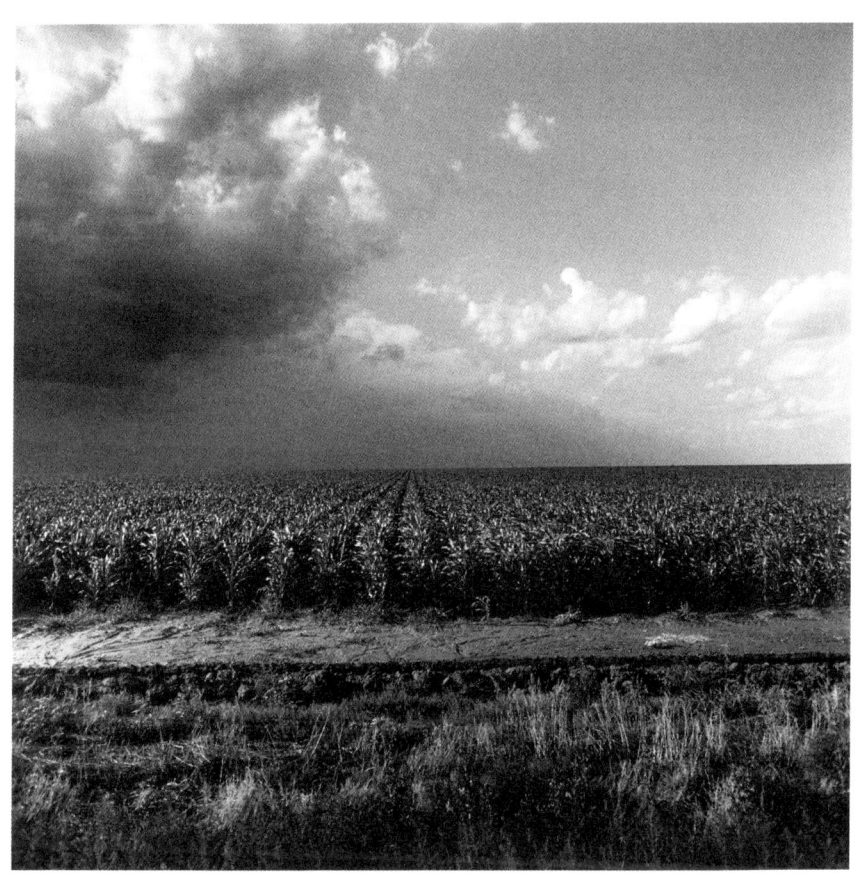

Frank Gohlke
American, born 1942
Landscape near Plainview, Texas
1975
Gelatin silver print
13⅞ × 13⅞ in. (35.2 × 35.2 cm)
2018.476

An-My Lê was born and grew up in Saigon, Vietnam. In the last days before the United States withdrew from the Vietnam War, in 1975, American embassy and military personnel evacuated then fifteen-year-old Lê and her family to the states. To better understand her feelings about her homeland, the war, and her sudden departure from everything she knew, Lê has spent twenty-five years photographing U.S. military subjects, visiting Vietnam to make landscapes and portraits, and documenting the lives of Vietnamese American fishermen and their families along the Gulf Coast. Taken as a whole, her work can be understood as a search for an accommodation with her personal history, with Vietnam's postwar history, and with American political, social, and military policy of the last fifty years.

The Thuận Thành district where Lê made this photograph held the ancient capital of Vietnam, Luy Lâu, and two of the most famous Buddhist temples in Vietnam: the Dâu Pagoda (187–226 CE) and the Bút Tháp Temple complex (1200s). Bút Tháp contains masterpieces of seventeenth-century woodcarving and a large statue of Avalokiteśvara, or Guanyin, revered as the embodiment of compassion. By choosing to photograph a more quotidian landscape nearby, Lê exchanged spectacle for a deep, layered look at contemporary Vietnam.

It appears that people are in the process of carrying bricks from the buildings in this picture and stacking them for removal to another building site. Soft light penetrates the moist air, illuminating a planted field in the foreground, a canal in the middle distance, and graceful trees and a horizon softened by smoke or atmospheric haze in the background. Time seems to hover.

EP

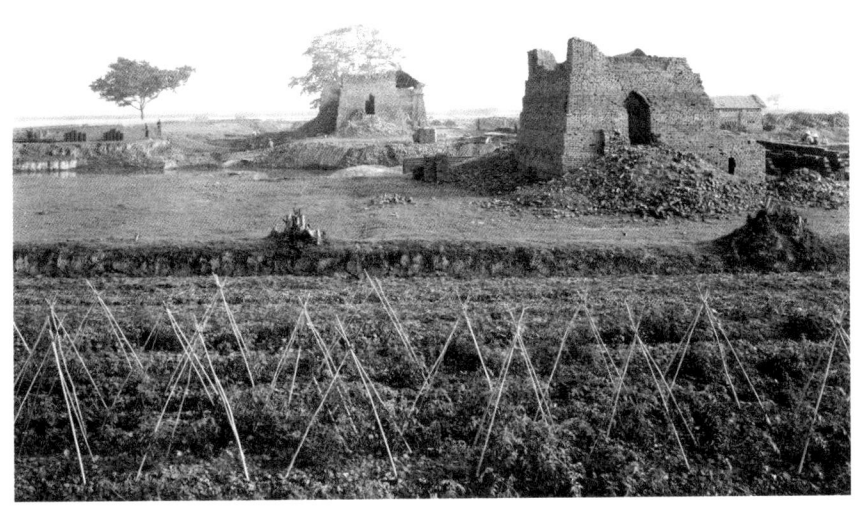

An-My Lê
American, born 1960 in Vietnam
Viêt Nam: Untitled, But Thap
1996
Gelatin silver print
9⅛ × 12⅞ in. (23.2 × 32.7 cm)
2018.503

Edward S. Curtis is best known for his sweeping photographic project, *The North American Indian*. Started in 1906 with seed money from the Wall Street powerhouse J. P. Morgan, that twenty-year project generated motion pictures, wax cylinder recordings, and more than 40,000 photographs intended to document and preserve the lifeways of North America's Indigenous people. The project filled twenty illustrated text volumes and twenty portfolios of large format photogravure prints. It bankrupted the photographer. Today, that work is both treasured and criticized for its romanticized image of Indigenous people.

Seven years before he embarked on his magnum opus, Curtis sailed to Alaska as the photographer for the Harriman Expedition. Financed by railroad magnate Edward Harriman, the expedition attracted such eminent figures as naturalist John Burroughs; C. Hart Merriam of the U.S. Biological Survey and his counterpart in geology, William H. Dall; and George Bird Grinnell, the editor of *Forest and Stream* magazine, whose editorializing rescued the last 200 bison in the United States. Perhaps the most notable member of the party was the Scottish-born naturalist and writer John Muir, the co-founder of the Sierra Club and a leading advocate of wilderness preservation. In 1879, Muir had been the first Euro-American to explore what is now Glacier Bay National Park; the glacier mentioned in the title of this photograph is named for him. In this Curtis photograph, a meandering river curves through the picture towards an arm of the sea glimpsed at the horizon. The steady flow of river water has cut through a glacial moraine to expose the still-standing trees of a forest buried unknown centuries ago. The eerie landscape nods to the depths of geological time and reminds viewers that ours is a world of constant change and rebirth.

EP

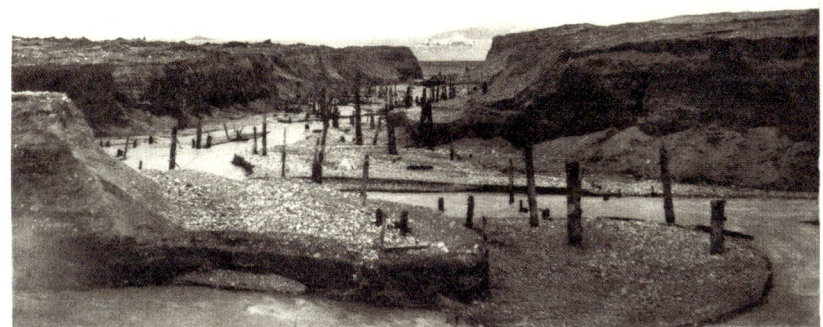

PHOTOGRAPH BY CURTIS RESURRECTED FOREST NEAR MUIR GLACIER JOHN ANDREW & SON

Edward S. Curtis
American, 1868–1952
Resurrected Forest near Muir Glacier
June 1899
Photogravure
4½ × 7¼ in. (11.4 × 18.4 cm)
2018.464

Almost since photography emerged in the 1830s, certain pictures have held talismanic power as reminders of significant people and experiences. Who hasn't treasured a portrait of a loved one, a picture from a gathering of friends, or a scene from a memorable trip? Because photographs remain fixed in time while the things they represent keep changing from the moment the shutter has snapped, every picture has the potential to carry us backward, or to measure how we—ourselves, our societies—might do things differently going forward.

This photograph is one that was mass-produced for sale to visitors to the World's Columbian Exposition in Chicago. More than 27 million people attended the exposition between May and October 1893, but one wouldn't know that from the emptiness and apparent silence of the exhibition hall. The photograph is an idealized version of the fair and a perfect keepsake that gives life to the experience without the noise and bustle of the throng. For some, a picture like this invited reflection.

The tree trunk in the picture is a small section of a giant sequoia that stood 300 feet tall before it was felled and sawn to pieces. Writing of the big trees in Sequoia National Park, John Muir said, "No description can give any adequate idea of their singular majesty, much less their beauty."[*] Removed from the forest, shipped from California to Chicago, and reassembled from mismatched pieces, the exhibited tree could not compare to meeting a living sequoia in its own habitat. Even so, the mounted specimen was as close as most Americans would ever come to an encounter with the real thing. Perhaps the photograph was an important reminder of how that felt. We cannot know what meaning this photograph held for the person who bought it. From today's perspective, the picture reflects nineteenth-century environmental values that conflict with environmental thought 130 years after the photographer set up the camera.

EP

---

[*] John Muir, "The Sequoia and General Grant National Parks," in *Our National Parks* (1901). The John Muir Exhibit, Sierra Club, https://vault.sierraclub.org/john_muir_exhibit/writings/our_national_parks/chapter_9.aspx.

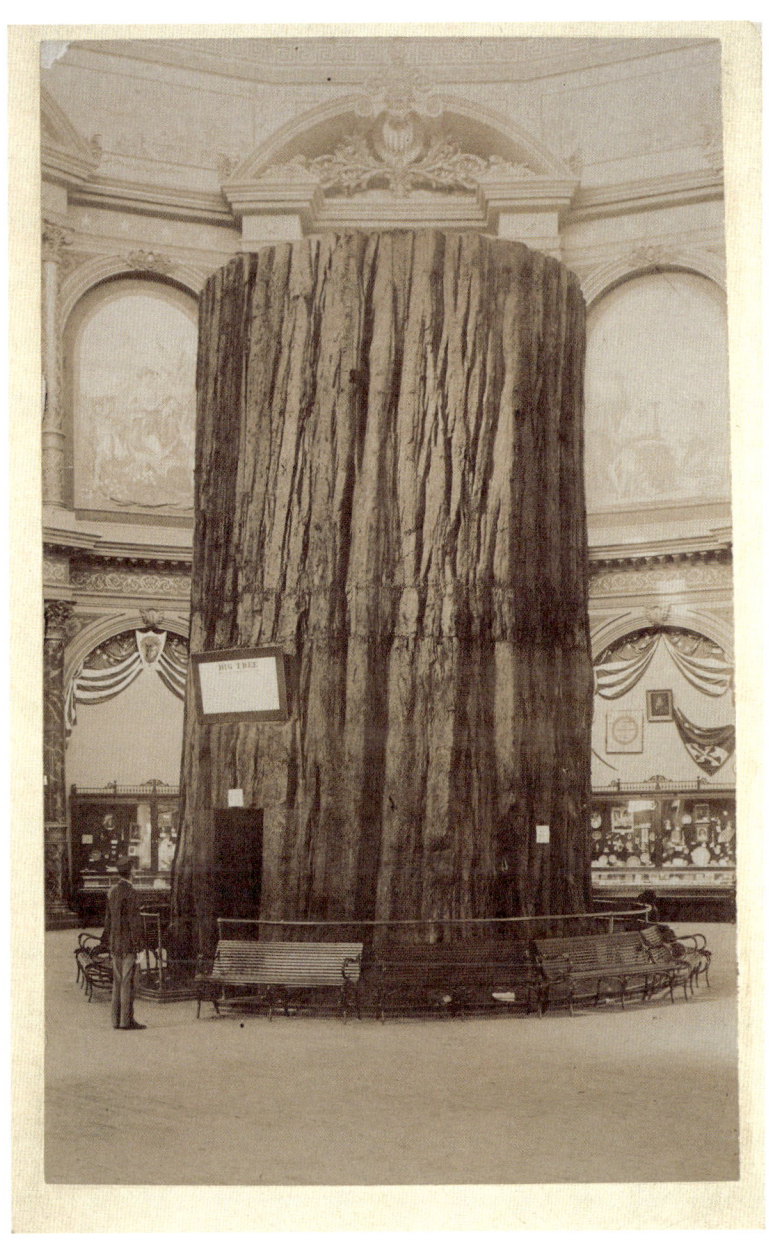

Unknown maker
Big Tree from the Sequoia National Park
1893
Albumen silver print
6⅛ × 3¾ in. (15.6 × 9.5 cm)
2018.562

Zsolt Kadar is inspired by the storytelling possibilities of art. For him, photography has the ability to show what exists in the world, and the photographer has the power to frame that reality in a way that highlights a particular aspect, such as finding a moment of beauty amid heartbreaking circumstances or the quiet amid chaos.

A sense of duality is demonstrated here in a picture that at a glance may appear to be children at play, but upon a closer look at the kids' gestures, expressions, and surroundings, the image takes on a more mysterious and foreboding tone. Two young children bundled in their winter clothes huddle together beneath a large, old tree with gnarled, cavernous roots. The darkness of night obscures the surroundings, while the artificial light of the camera flash illuminates a scene of children gazing upward with a mix of curiosity and concern at some-thing we cannot see. The bare branches, fallen leaves, and dusting of snow in the shadows of the background suggest this photograph was made on a winter's night.

It is not clear why these children are out at night alone when they should be home in bed. Instead, this picture expresses a sense of vulnerability that all humans can relate to. The children are dwarfed by the natural world that surrounds them, emphasizing its powerful force which serves as both shelter from and potentially the source of danger implied in the picture. *Clari and David, Friedberg, DE* is part of Kadar's series *Le Mal du Pays* which translates to homesickness. Kadar was born in Nagyvàrad, Transylvania, a region in Romania, but has been based in the United States since the 1980s, so reflecting on changing notions of home is likely familiar to him. The feelings of uncertainty, disconnection, and longing for comfort and stability that are bound up in the idea of homesickness are powerfully demonstrated in this image.

KR

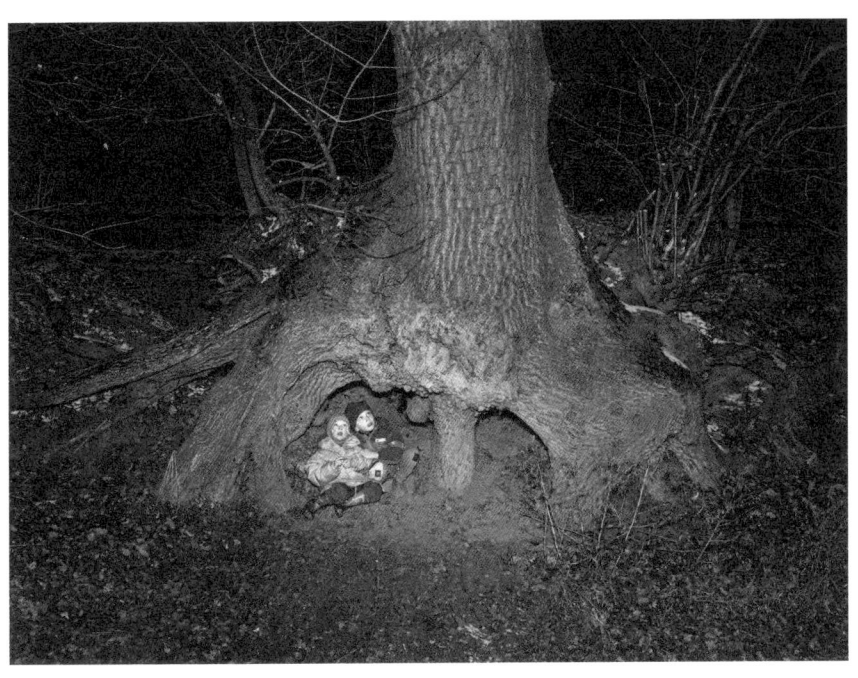

Zsolt Kadar
American, born in Nagyvárad, Transylvania (present-day Romania) in 1966
Clari and David, Friedberg, DE
2000
Gelatin silver print
11⅜ × 15⅜ in. (28.9 × 39.1 cm)
2018.501

Linda Connor has traveled and photographed extensively on six continents to explore places she describes as "steeped in the passage of time and resonant with spirituality."* In the process, she has created landscapes of great intimacy and emotional power that blur our usual intellectual boundaries between different cultures and historical eras.

Working in Canyon de Chelly on the Navajo Reservation in 1987, Connor encountered this breathtaking monument to nature's mysterious force. Struck by lightning and burned to its heartwood, this tree seems as animated in death as it must have been in life. Rising from sparse grass and slabs of sandstone at the foot of a cliff, the tree takes on the form of an otherworldly creature with its wings (or arms) spread. It could be making a warning gesture or about to take flight, or it could be just a surprising and remarkable remnant of an event that is lost to time.

A lightning strike is a powerful metaphor. Some religions view lightning bolts as forms of divine punishment. A more positive, less fearful perspective sees them as symbols of spiritual illumination or of a step in nature's unending process of destruction and renewal. Connor's photograph so entrances us with its questions that it hardly needs to provide answers.

EP

* *Odyssey: The Photographs of Linda Connor*, July 2–October 30, 2010, Rhode Island School of Design Museum, https://risdmuseum.org/exhibitions-events/exhibitions/odyssey.

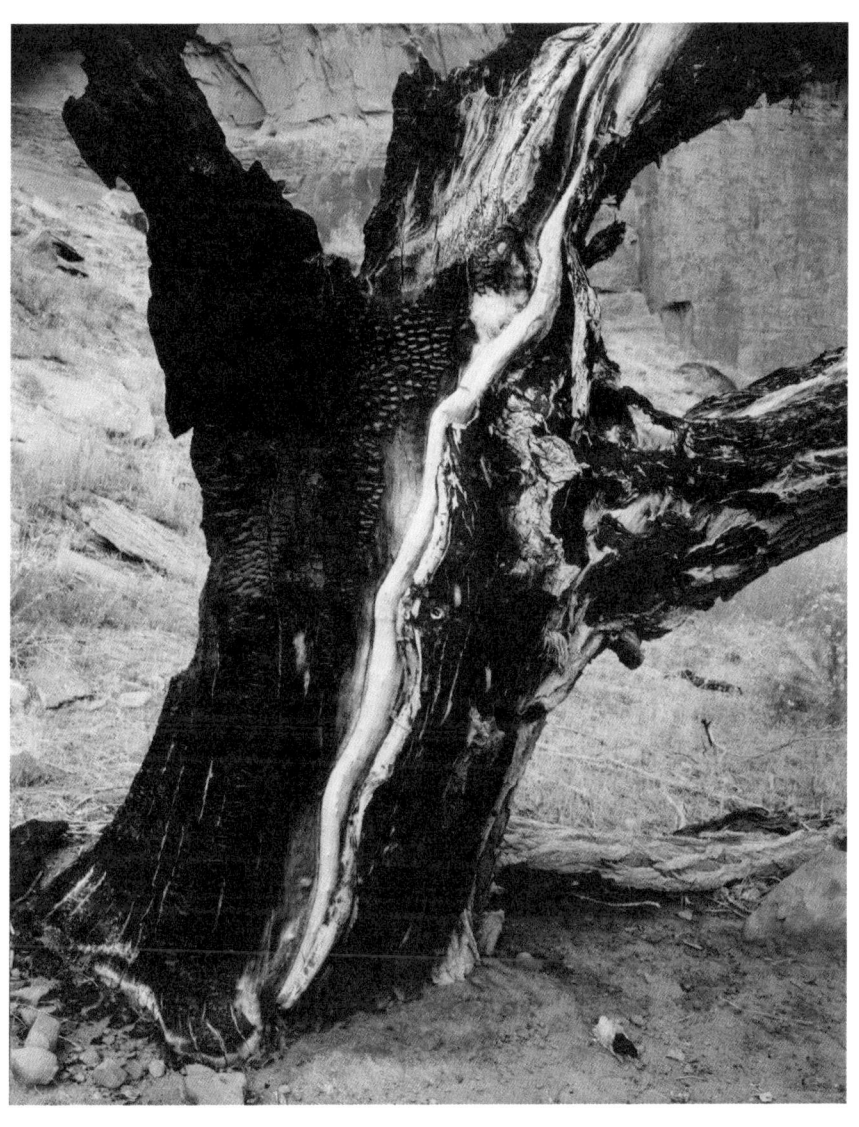

Linda Connor
American, born 1944
Lightning Tree, Canyon de Chelly, Arizona
1987
Toned gelatin silver print
10 × 8 in. (25.4 × 20.3 cm)
2018.457

There was a staggering, if unacknowledged, need in the late 1960s and '70s for a fresh, uncompromising photographic reexamination of the landscape of the American West. While Robert Adams's 1974 publication, *The New West*, ostensibly gave us an unexpected look at suburban development along Colorado's Front Range, its true subject, Adams wrote in his introduction to the photographs, is "not tract homes or freeways but the source of all Form, light."* The light in this undertaking was characterized, by high key, predominantly white tones rather than the luminous or evocative atmosphere associated with traditional landscape photography.

Nevertheless, Adams's affection for values of traditional photography was brought home to me when, after we had both contributed texts to the 1984 *Aperture* issue, "Minor White: A Living Remembrance," he invited me to visit him in Colorado and subsequently asked me if I'd like to exchange prints. One of the images he chose was the picture of the Intihuatana altar at Machu Picchu, which I had made in 1971. As an exchange student in Peru between 1964 and 1965, I had photographed at Machu Picchu and other Inca sites with the 35 mm format, but by 1971 I had resolved to work in depth at Inca sites with the large format camera.

On one occasion at Machu Picchu that year, I awoke to find the site shrouded in mist. Anxious to see how the subdued light might help me photograph the Intihuatana stone, I went directly to the high outcrop on which it is located. Working quickly in the wet, soft light allowed me to isolate the altar from its dramatic setting—instead of seeing a dark river gorge behind it, the shape of the altar was clearly defined against a white backdrop. As the clouds began to break up, delicate tones of white and gray emerged in the clouds, and I was given a moment of unforgettable picture making. Light, whether dramatic, austere, or gentle, as Robert Adams suggests, remains our truest, most enduring photographic subject: whether it illuminates an ancient altar or perishable shelters along Colorado's front range.

Edward Ranney

* Robert Adams, *The New West: Landscapes Along the Colorado Front Range* (Boulder: The Colorado Associated University Press, 1974), xii.

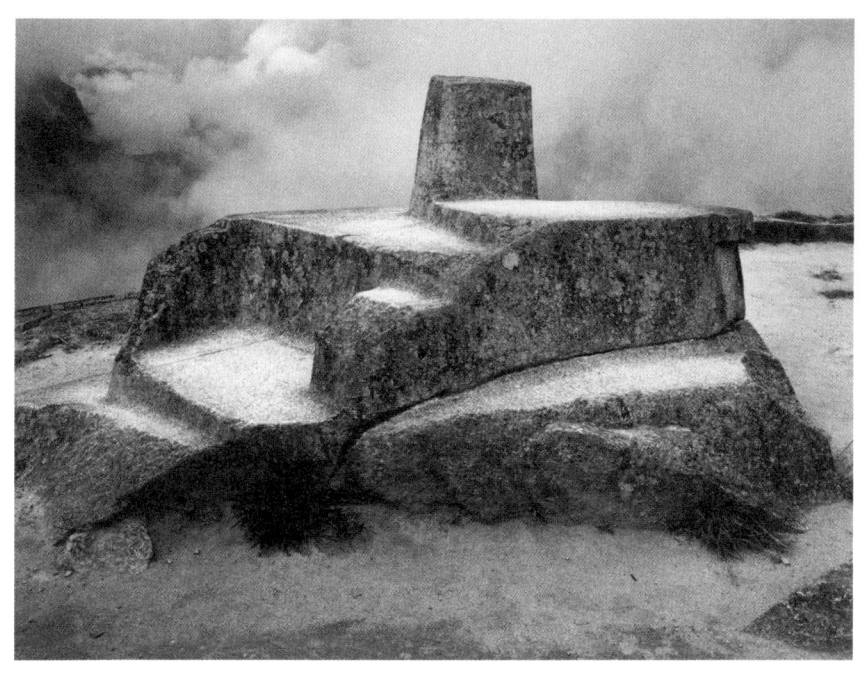

Edward Ranney
American, born 1942
Intihuatana, Machu Picchu, Peru
1971
Gelatin silver print
8¾ × 12⅛ in. (22.2 × 30.8 cm)
2018.520

Lois Conner prefers a wooden camera built around 1910 that makes seven-by-seven inch film negatives—eighty-eight times the size of a single 35 mm frame. One sees pictures of groups in banquet halls or lined up on a sidewalk that were made with cameras like hers. It is a recalcitrant tool that gets heavier with the added weight of a tripod, a lens, and wooden holders for individual sheets of film. Although Conner has used her camera for intimate portraits at close distances, she is a landscape photographer first and foremost. She thinks nothing of turning the camera on its side to make scroll-shaped vertical pictures like this one.

Making a photograph with a big camera can be a drawn-out, painstaking business. Minute adjustments are necessary to frame a picture, to bring it into focus, and to expose the film correctly. One often has to wait for the wind to die down or for an errant cloud or rubbernecker to get out of the way. A crowd of onlookers gathered to watch Conner as she worked to make this picture. When she judged that everything was right and turned to pick up the film holder she would insert into the camera, a collective gasp from the audience warned her in time to whirl around, see the front leg of her tripod sinking, and catch her camera before it tumbled over the precipice. She tightened the tripod leg, started over, and finished what she set out to do.

One can hope one's photographs will stand apart from, and be better than, the tales one can spin about making them. Conner regrouped from her narrow escape to make this serene and powerful photograph of the Leshan Giant Buddha, an immense seated figure carved from solid sandstone between 713 and 803. Looking down, we see only one of the statue's hands and one of its feet. Across the defile, a 200-foot stairway winds from the valley floor to the statue's eye level. Thick bushes tumble over the rock faces, and a row of trees flows in silhouette down the skyline. We cannot see the entire figure of Buddha, yet his tranquil presence is manifest in Conner's photo.

EP

Lois Conner
American, born 1951
Leshan, Sichuan, China
1986
Platinum/palladium print
16¾ × 6⅜ in. (42.5 × 16.2 cm)
2018.564

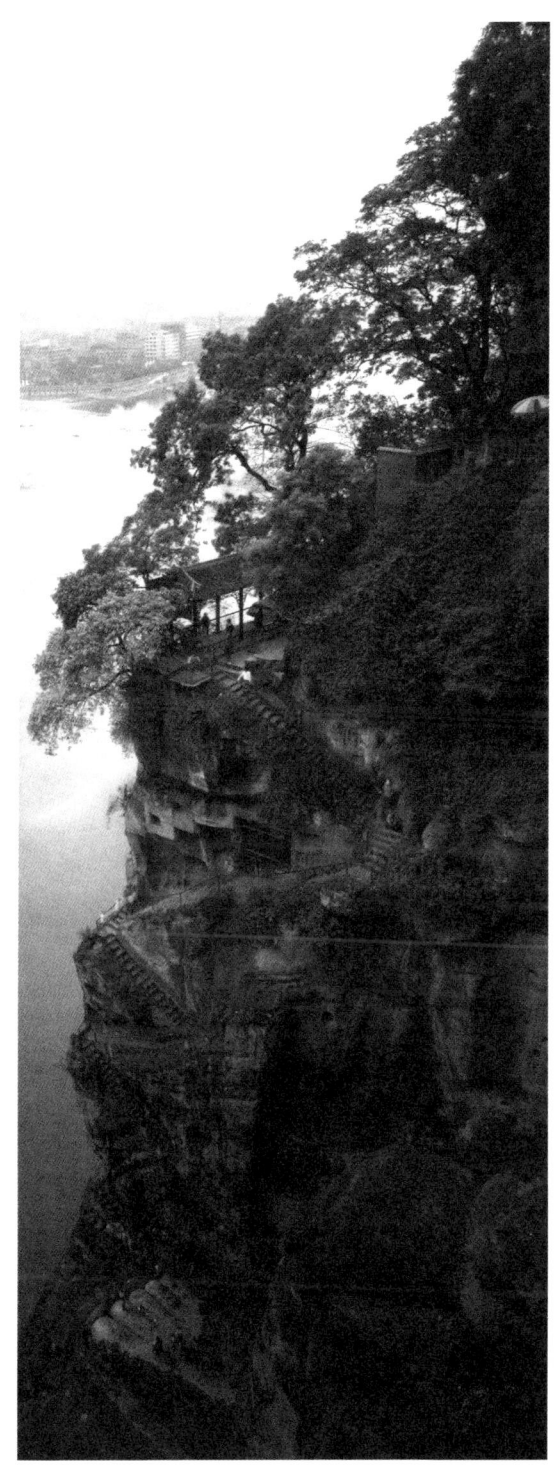

Mary Peck refined her eye and perfected her technique while assisting the photographers Paul Caponigro and Laura Gilpin in Santa Fe in the 1970s. Peck has practiced quietly since that time, immersing herself in long-term projects that grow from her love of nature, her curiosity about the spiritual lives of societies not her own, and her calm faith in photography's capacity to bear witness. Among many things, she has photographed the temples of ancient Greece, the ancient cultural center of Chaco Canyon, the Olympic Peninsula's Elwah River, and of course the tiny Asian nation of Bhutan.

Peck traveled in Bhutan several times in the early 2000s and eventually won permission to stay beyond the strict limits of a standard Bhutanese tourist visa. She was able to visit remote parts of the country where trekkers and even aid workers seldom go. Through her travels she found deep respect for Bhutanese social and religious traditions and came to believe that a nation that measures "gross national happiness" instead of GDP has much to teach the developed world. In her book, *Bhutan: Between Heaven and Earth*, Peck wrote, "what I saw in Bhutan was a landscape and culture that reminded me of Wallace Stegner's personal expression of faith in the importance of geography, and especially wilderness, to human personality and culture. Calling wilderness 'the geography of hope,' Stegner dreamed of a day when those in the American West would 'create a society to match its scenery.' Bhutan was reassuring in its wholeness." * This string of prayer flags, worn and faded to gossamer against a forest backdrop, speaks to a constant and mindful relationship with nature that lies at the core of what Stegner had in mind.

EP

* Mary Peck, "Bhutan's Curve of Time," in *Bhutan: Between Heaven and Earth* (Santa Fe: Merlin Press and Phoenix Art Museum, 2014), n.p.

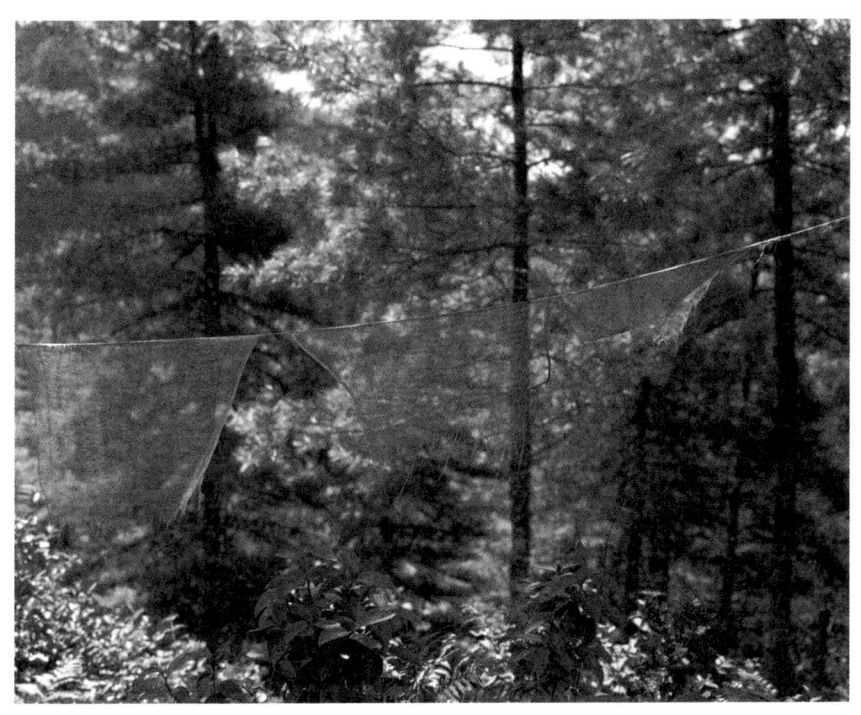

Mary Peck
American, born 1952
Prayer Flags, Taktsang, Bhutan
1999
Gelatin silver print
7¼ × 9 in. (18.4 × 22.9 cm)
2018.518

The photographs were made in Morris's orchard perched on top of a limestone bluff along the Mississippi River where I grew up. Morris and his wife, Judy, had given me permission to photograph where his family had grown apples for generations.

I wanted to work here because this orchard was a bit wild, with old trees, not overly pruned, not perfect. There is something humbly heroic about their determined nature to bud, flower, fruit, wither, and rest for the next cycle of life, perhaps for a hundred years.

The steep, winding gravel road reminded me that this place, my childhood home along the river, is orchard country. (It is here in Minnesota that the beloved Honeycrisp apple was hybridized.) Around our kitchen table, "apple speak" with family friends was common: of bees, frost dates, crop damage, new cider, best pie apple, local pickers, and dreaded hail damage that affected the yearly income of families.

In September among Morris's trees, the grasses had grown tall, mixed with wild purple asters, red sumac, and prairie sage. The ticks were gone. When I asked to come, Morris always said yes except when he was spraying, perhaps knowing that this pesticide is toxic. Sadly, I found out later that as I was making these photographs, his funeral was in progress. This piece has always had great poignancy for me.

The photograph was sent to Robert in a moment of shy bravado. A lover of choral music, I think that as art makers we may be in the same chorus—one with solo tenors, sopranos, basses and mezzos, and a whole cast of us singing harmonies.

The prolific writings, books, and photographs of Robert Adams have been to me like a rock of understanding about landscape, especially those where one's feet have traveled the same trail often—not an itinerant response—landscapes in which one gains understanding with familiarity or communion over time. His wisdom, generosity, and original thinking has helped me with my own artistic questions about why and where and, as he poses in elegant simplicity in his essays: "What can help?" My response is, well, *you* do.

Linda Gammell

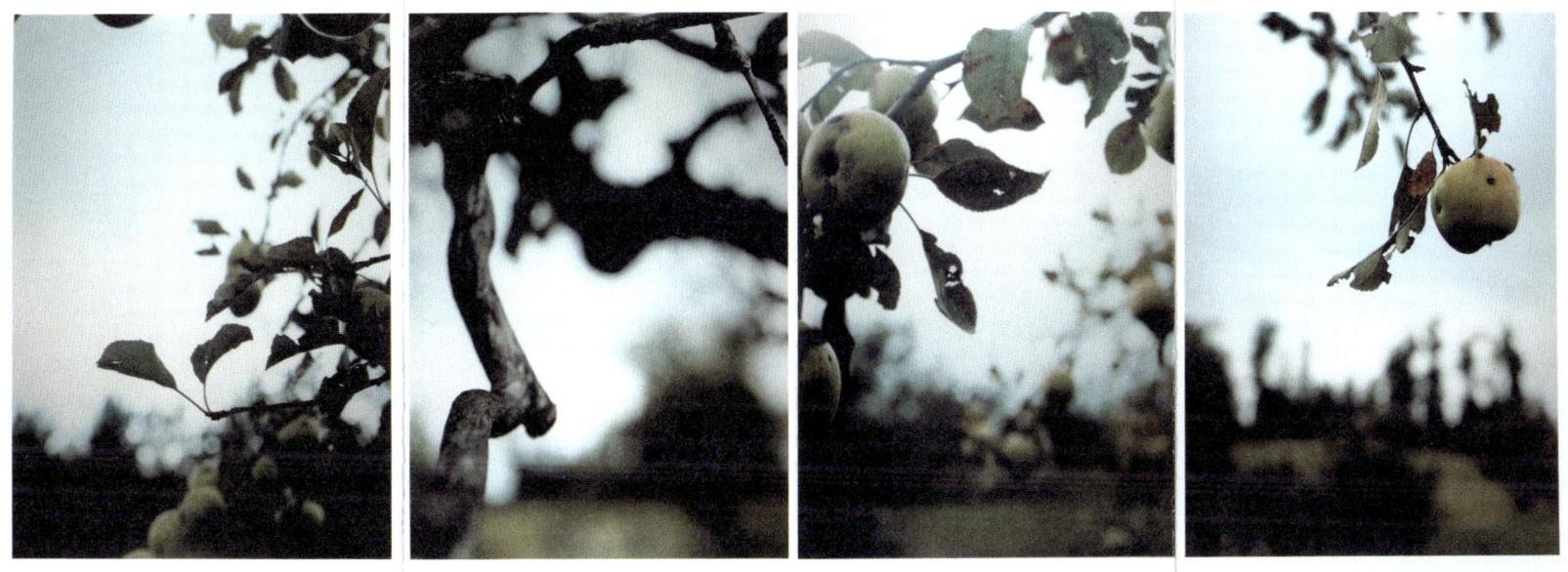

for Bork & Kerstin

orchard/September (for Morris)

Linda Gammell
American, born 1948
Orchard, September (for Morris)
2012
Inkjet prints
Overall 4¾ × 14½ in. (12.1 × 36.8 cm)
2018.473

Akiyoshi Taniguchi became interested in photography as a child growing up in his family's Buddhist temple and made pictures throughout his teens. Upon graduating high school, he wanted to see and experience the world beyond what he knew. Taniguchi went to New York City in 1979 where he spent the next five years immersing himself in photography and music. While there, he studied with photographer Leo Rubinfien (p. 49) and made pictures of friends and acquaintances in their apartments. Taniguchi left New York for Los Angeles to study at a Buddhist temple before returning to Japan. Today, he is head priest at Chohouin Buddhist Temple of Kuramae, Tokyo, like many generations of his family have been before.

Photography and Buddhism have been interconnected throughout his life. As Taniguchi made pictures and looked at and collected the pictures of other photographers, he began to see the act of making or experiencing a photograph as a form of meditation. In 2006, he opened Kurenboh, a small photography gallery on the temple grounds designed for meditation that is open to the public and intended to be experienced by one person at a time.

There is a meditative quality to this picture that creates a space for contemplation and reflection—the longer one looks, the more one sees. Taniguchi made this photograph when he was just seventeen years old, right before he moved to New York. With that in mind, this picture becomes infused with a sense of longing, dreaming, and curiosity of what lies on the other side of the sea.

At a glance, the view may feel expansive, appearing almost like an illuminated city at night viewed from a plane overhead. Look again and an intimate view of a glistening seascape at night comes into focus. Patches of seafoam float in between specks of light brilliantly shimmering on the surface of the moving water. There is no horizon line in this image, and the shoreline, likely just below the bottom of the frame, remains out of view. The result is a picture that encourages the eye and the mind to ponder what lies beyond the frame or within ourselves.

KR

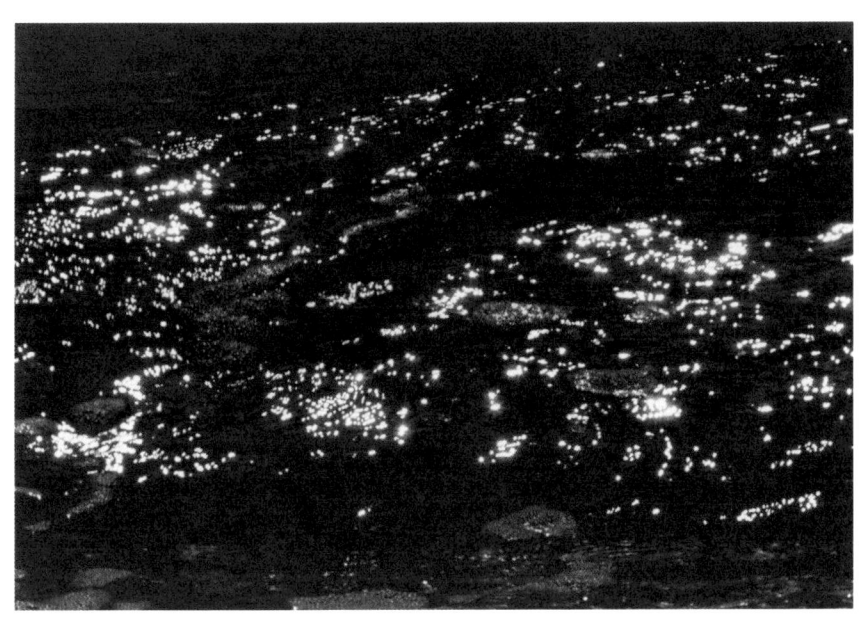

Akiyoshi Taniguchi
Japanese, born 1960
The Sea
1978
Gelatin silver print
7 × 10¼ in. (17.8 × 26 cm)
2018.573

While you and John were talking" is the inscription I wrote on the back of the photograph. John Gossage and I were driving from San Diego to Washington, DC, on a leisurely two-week honeymoon trip. This day, exactly September 9, 1992, we had driven north up Colorado's Front Range to visit Bob and Kerstin where they lived in Longmont. It was my first meeting, and I was beyond excited, nervous, as Bob's written words and his work were my North Star. September is my favorite month in the West with wild sunflowers lining the roads and the light beginning to angle low. As we drove into town, I saw many tall, dark red hollyhocks everywhere, in all the in-between spaces. Bob answered the door, ready for us, and we sat in the light-filled rooms of their house. Bob's slow, warm voice immediately had me at ease. We were there for hours. We spent time talking about his thought process, preparation, and printing for his work, which included at that moment *Listening to the River*. John and Bob continued to talk (and all of it was quite interesting), but I kept remembering the hollyhocks and knew there were some not far from the house. I went to go find them with Bob's good wishes. This image was taken there, bracketed by conversation. I sent it to him soon after, a sort of commemoration of our first meeting. What I did not know is our friendship had just begun, and it continues in much the way he speaks—slowly, easily, with warmth.

Terri Weifenbach

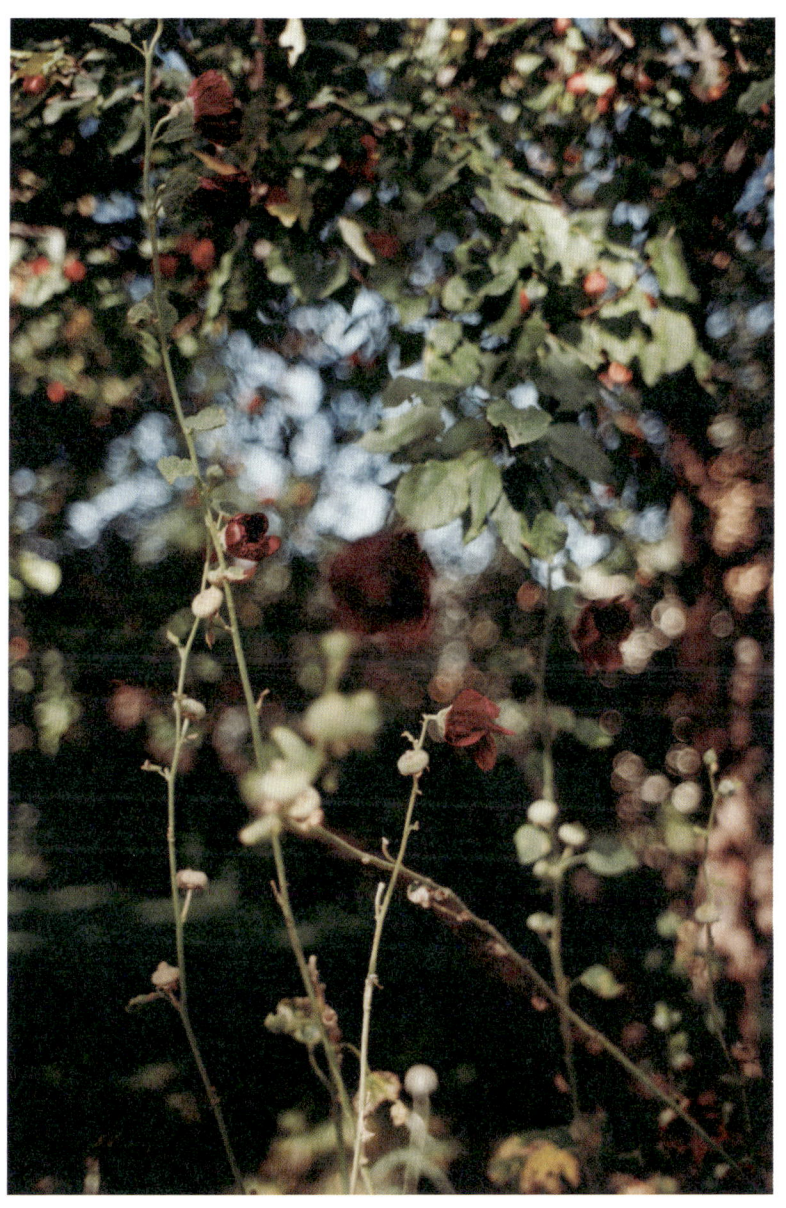

Terri Weifenbach
American, born 1957
While you and John were talking . . .
September 9, 1992
Chromogenic color print
7¼ × 4⅞ in. (18.4 × 12.4 cm)
2018.555

AFTERWORD

Photography is essentially an act of sharing. Photographers discover in the finders of their cameras something so needed that they often end up giving prints away. I have been the recipient of this generosity, and the pictures, like some paintings at the Denver Art Museum that I still remember from my youth, have gone on to reinforce in me a sense of consequence and possibility.

I also value these gifts for what they tell me about those who made them. Consider, for example, the *caring* of the person who pictured the child amid trash in Tijuana (p. 51). This was not a subject at the time that was likely to excite elements of the art world.

Note, too, the *honesty* about our probable future that brought a photographer to record the inhuman scale of New York skyscrapers and another picture maker to single out a prehistoric wasp next to the wheel of a junked vehicle (p. 61 and 67).

And consider the *hope* that must have inspired someone—a mother or father?—to picture two young women, standing straight, by a windmill and the remains of a blizzard (p. 21).

Observe as well the *openness to the unknown* (and to laughter) that enabled a photographer to set up a large camera on a tripod in a school room, to compose a picture on the ground glass, and then impulsively to make the exposure as the composition disintegrated while the children had fun (p. 53).

Not least, consider the *alertness* to beauty—to small, red flowers and sunstruck leaves—that allowed a photographer to find in a characteristic American suburb a revelation (p. 103).

All of which was done so that the rest of us might live with the hope of some assurance. When columnist Mark Shields retired from PBS *Newshour*, he spoke of a blessing for which I too am grateful: "Everyone of us has been warmed by fires we did not build, and every one of us has drunk from wells we did not dig."[*]

Robert Adams
Astoria, Oregon, 2020

[*] Mark Shields, "Shields and Brooks Celebrate a Lifetime in American Politics," December 18, 2020, PBS *Newshour,* https://www.pbs.org/newshour/show/shields-and-brooks-celebrate-a-lifetime-in-american-politics.

ARTISTS IN THE COLLECTION

The Robert and Kerstin Adams Collection includes 163 objects (159 photographs, 2 drawings, 1 etching, and 1 sculpture) by several unknown makers and the following artists:

Ken Abbott
Robert Adams
Lewis Baltz
Richard Benson
Pierre Bonnard
Mathew Brady
Daniel Cheek
Mark Cohen
Lois Conner
Linda Connor
Edward S. Curtis
Peter Henry Emerson
Chuck Forsman
Lucian Freud
Lee Friedlander
Linda Gammell
Frank Gohlke
Anthony Hernandez
C. A. Hickman
Bill Jay
Zsolt Kadar
Yousuf Karsh
Charles J. Katz Jr.
Stuart Klipper
Suzanne Lafont
An-My Lê
Jack Lueders-Booth
Afonso Malato de Sousa

Steve Maxwell
A. J. Meek
Nicholas Nixon
Dorothy Norman
Eric Paddock
Mary Peck
Edward Ranney
Judith Joy Ross
Leo Rubinfien
Mark Ruwedel
Michael Schmidt
Richard Serra
Mike Smith
J. W. Souder
Mark Steenerson
David Stephenson
Paul Strand
Alfred Stieglitz
Akiyoshi Taniguchi
Bob Thall
Jerry L. Thompson
Carl Van Vechten
Terri Weifenbach
Edward Weston
Dennis Witmer
William Wylie
Marcos Zimmermann

CONTRIBUTING AUTHORS

Robert Adams
Photographer based in Astoria, Oregon, and along with his wife, Kerstin, donor of this collection

Linda Gammell
Photographer based in Saint Paul, Minnesota

Frank Gohlke
Photographer based in Tucson, Arizona

Eric Paddock (EP)
Curator of Photography, Denver Art Museum

Edward Ranney
Photographer based in Santa Fe, New Mexico

Kimberly Roberts (KR)
Senior Curatorial Assistant, Photography, Denver Art Museum

Terri Weifenbach
Photographer based in Paris, France

IMAGE CREDITS

Published on the occasion of *Other People's Pictures: Selections from the Robert and Kerstin Adams Collection,* curated by Eric Paddock

Organized by the Denver Art Museum
August 28, 2022–February 26, 2023

The Denver Art Museum thanks the residents who support the Scientific and Cultural Facilities District (SCFD).

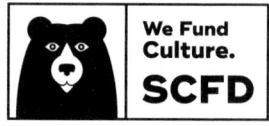

© 2022 Denver Art Museum

Denver Art Museum
100 West 14th Avenue Parkway
Denver, CO 80204
denverartmuseum.org

Distributed by University of Oklahoma Press
2800 Venture Drive
Norman, OK 73069
oupress.com

The Denver Art Museum is located on the homeland of the Arapaho, Cheyenne, and Ute people, along with many people from other Indigenous nations that call this place home. Learn more about our commitments to better represent, elevate, and support Indigenous cultures and people, past and present, on our website.

ISBN 978-1-945483-11-0
Library of Congress Cataloging-in-Publication Data
Names: Denver Art Museum, author, issuing body. | Paddock, Eric, curator.
Title: Companion to the Robert and Kerstin Adams photography collection at the Denver Art Museum / contributing authors: Robert Adams, Linda Gammell, Frank Gohlke, Edward Ranney, Eric Paddock, EP, Edward Ranney, Kimberly Roberts, KR, Terri Weifenbach.
Description: Denver, CO : Denver Art Museum, [2022] | Includes bibliographical references. | Summary: "Published on the occasion of the exhibition of the Robert and Kerstin Adams Collection at the Denver Art Museum"-- Provided by publisher.
Identifiers: LCCN 2021043396 | ISBN 9781945483110 (paperback)
Subjects: LCSH: Photography, Artistic--Exhibitions. | Denver Art Museum--Exhibitions. | Adams, Robert, 1937---Photograph collections--Exhibitions. | Adams, Kerstin--Photograph collections--Exhibitions. | Photograph collections--Colorado--Denver--Exhibitions.
Classification: LCC TR655 .D46 2022 | DDC 770.74/78883--dc23/eng/20211005
LC record available at https://lccn.loc.gov/2021043396

Editor: Valerie Hellstein
Senior Curatorial Assistant: Kimberly Roberts
Managing Editor: Kati Woock
Manager of Photographic Services: Christina Jackson
Additional photography: Jeff Wells and Eric Stephenson
Manager of Rights and Reproductions: Renée Miller
Design by Mary Junda, Junda Graphics, Denver

Printed and bound by Shapco Printing, Inc., Minneapolis

All dimensions are image dimensions, h × w, unless otherwise noted.

Cover: Terri Weifenbach, *While you and John were talking . . .*, p. 103
Back cover: Unknown maker, Real Photo Postcard (Boy, Dog, Tug-o-war), p. 21

Unless otherwise indicated, images are courtesy of and in the permanent collection of the Denver Art Museum.

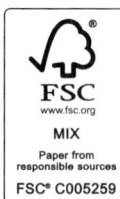